PROFIT HIKER

PROFIT HIKER

11 TRAILS TO GAIN
LASTING ELEVATION
IN YOUR BUSINESS

BY SIMON TRASK

ProfitHiker.com

ISBN: 979-8-9905723-0-0
E-Book ISBN: 979-8-9905723-1-7
Audio Book ISBN: 979-8-9905723-2-4

Scripture references are from: THE HOLY BIBLE,
NEW INTERNATIONAL VERSION®, NIV® Copyright © 1973,
1978, 1984, 2011 by Biblica, Inc.® Used by permission.
All rights reserved worldwide.

Edited by Courtney Cohen
Cover, design, and layout by Simon Trask
Photography by Bill Trask and Brandon Jones

Contents

Acknowledgements

Thank You first to the Creator of the universe, who gave me the idea for this book, and kept the words flowing.

Thanks to my loving and ever-supportive wife Cindy who has been supportive of every wild and seemingly impossible idea I have brought to our family. If everyone had a Cindy Trask in their life, this world would truly be a different place.

Also, thanks to Steve and Courtney Cohen of Now Found Publishing who really helped to bring this book to life.

This book was written for small business owners everywhere, the true heart and soul of every community.

Introduction

I had it all, and I wasn't happy.

It all started in November of 2016. Fall is unequivocally my favorite time of year. The seasons are changing, the mornings are crisp, and there is a certain contentment in the air. Everyone looks forward to the fun outdoor events in our area: football season, music festivals, harvest celebrations, and, of course, the State Fair of Texas. Fall is also peak hunting season; so there is an added excitement and anticipation for what lies ahead. The holidays are on the horizon, and I look forward to having fun with our children. While I do appreciate each season with its own personality, and I do especially long for the changing of the seasons, Fall is special.

But this year was different.

Our third child had just been born, and I was now a "Girl Dad." We had two boys and a girl, all under the age of four. Other dads had shared all throughout my wife's pregnancy that raising daughters is different, and you'll never be the same. I didn't understand what they meant, because not long after her birth I jumped right back into work, back into the business that "needed me."

On paper, my business partner and I had built a successful business. We had tripled the revenue of our advertising agency in our first five years together and had assembled a fantastic team of very talented people doing work that we were all proud of. We were at the top of the field in our town and growing the business in new ways. Starting as a web design firm, we had scaled to full-service advertising campaigns. This meant that we were spending six-figure advertising budgets on behalf of our clients and producing high quality television commercials for local businesses. I was at the center of some challenging and creative work, which is what puts wind in my sails. I was also making the best money I had ever made. This was all more than I ever thought I would have when I first became a graphic designer.

And I was not happy.

When the clocks changed from Daylight Savings to Standard Time as it does that first full weekend in November, it became more and more difficult. Every morning I would leave for work in the dark while all of my kids slept and come home in the dark with my new baby girl already asleep again. I would have dinner with my wife and two boys, spend a little time with them, and then put them to bed. I knew we had a baby in the house because I would see the case of diapers empty itself more and more each day. And, of course, there were the weekends with her – but I felt like my life was backwards. I had been telling myself that I was building this business for them. This would level up our family and give my kids a better kicking-off point for their lives, like my father did for us, and his father did for them. This mentality began to lose its footing as I allowed myself to ask the question, "What does it really mean to be a good dad?"

Over the coming months, I became very disenchanted with work. I tried to keep my spirits up, but all I could think about was that my baby girl, who we thought would be our youngest child for good, was going to grow up with even less of her father present than our boys got to experience. I chalked it up to the "Baby Blues" for the first few months, but I knew what was really happening in my heart: familiarity had bred contempt. It's funny how humanity can change so much from one century or millennium to the next, but some essential qualities like this remain that make us so very human. I had grown to resent the very house that I had helped build, the house that I now felt was keeping me from what I deeply wanted. When my partner and I first merged our independent businesses, I did not have any children. If there was a big pitch due, I could pull an all-nighter without much consequence. My wife is a medical professional and was often working third shift anyhow during that season of life. But kids change everything.

Fast forward to springtime, when I walked into my partner's office and handed him an offer to buy me out at ten cents on the dollar. After weeks and weeks of discussions with my loving wife, sleepless nights filled with endless questions, and a constant low-level anxiety I couldn't shake, I decided that we needed a big change. My partner asked for three weeks to consider the offer. In the end, he decided that he too was ready for a big change in life, and that we should try to sell the business together.

That was both unexpected and a major relief for me. I knew that it would be some time before we got any serious offers to consider, and I expected quite a bit of work in preparation for selling, but there was an end in sight.

Selling a business isn't necessarily a good thing or a bad thing in itself. These transactions happen every day for a variety of reasons, but often a major life event triggers the decision. Ideally the business is so good to you, why would you sell it? A business requires battling so much inertia to grow, and a business owner pours their heart and soul into that process. It can be like selling a child. In fact, when we got serious about selling, our accountant gave us a pep talk. He was a mentor figure for me during that process and in the years after. He asked us if "giving up and selling" was the story we wanted to tell. It was a very moving conversation, and full of love and wisdom for us in that moment, but even then, I just couldn't bring myself to stick it out any longer. I was completely burned out.

Jump ahead again once more to October of 2017, four days short of my daughter's first birthday. It was closing day, and we met with our company's new owner and the business broker at our attorney's office in a high rise building in downtown Fort Worth, Texas to sign the papers. I had a few weeks left in my obligation to help transition the new owner into the business, and I felt a tremendous sense of relief. The next year of rebooting my life was full of uncertainly, and we were financially negative every month for the next year. Eventually we stabilized and I was able to clearly see the path to redesign my life as a heavily involved dad.

In the following years of working independently and with other partners on various projects, I can't help but wonder what I missed out on by leaving the ad agency business. Knowing what I know now about leadership, I regret not fully owning my leadership role in the team. I never saw myself as a leader until I wasn't in that role any longer. With more than a decade of parenting under my belt now and a deeper understanding of what it means to lead, I think we really could have built a great organization if we had stuck with it. I do miss working with my team, and all of the energizing creative brainstorming sessions that were a part of weekly life in the advertising world. I took the easy offramp instead of the hard-but-good trail up the mountain.

I no longer have the opportunity to know what that advertising agency could have been had I committed to redesigning the business to fit my evolving home life rather than selling out and walking away. But you, as a business owner, still have the unique ability to reshape your business right here and now. You can tailor your business to your goals and values.

It all starts with profit.

A Mindset For Every Business

What is Profit Hiker?

Profit Hiker is a program to help business owners discover hidden profit, create margin, and avoid financial struggle. Small business is the lifeblood of every local community, and my mission is to help small business owners create margin, so you have a healthier business, employees, customers, community, and self. Profit Hiker was created to equip small business owners by giving you a trail map to better business health. I have personally used Profit Hiker to scale two of my businesses over 1,000% each, while maintaining good margins.

During my career, I have been invited behind the curtain of hundreds of small businesses—at least 400 by last count. I have talked face-to-face with small business owners who don't know what to do next to save their business, to grow their business, or to save themselves from inevitable burnout or even financial ruin. What I have come to realize is that business owners can usually rattle off a few really good ways to grow that they've already been thinking about. But if asked to write down a half dozen or more, they often hit a wall. What if they had a set of trail maps to navigate the wilderness of their future and be able to build enough margin in their business to get back to the passion that got them started?

When two small business owners come together (often over beverages), they either talk about common challenges or discuss new ways to grow. I have been a part of too many of these conversations to count. The heart of most small business owners is to create a healthy business for themselves, their customers, employees, and community. But where do you even start?

In the advertising agency business, I used to tell my team that, deep down, every single client who walks through our door wants *more*. They want to grow by getting more of something – usually it was pretty evident, like leads or sales or customers. But sometimes it was more subtle than that: they want to be the top dog in town, they want to send their kids to a better school, or engage more people in the community. What I came to realize is that while marketing is certainly valuable, we were only one of many opportunities that a small business could leverage to get "more." In fact, when asked to speak at a conference geared for small business owners, I deeply researched the topic and discovered there are actually 11 different approaches to creating better profit. Within those 11 approaches, there are a seemingly endless number of tactics a business owner can implement to create better margin.

Burnout is a common story among business owners; you are passionate about your skills and serving people, so you set out to change your community by being the best there is. The thing starts to work. You start growing, start hiring, get a bigger space – all the while having to blaze new or unexpected trails (often without a map). You are managing people and their personalities, developing operations, dealing with customers, putting out fires, driving new sales, all while trying to continue inspiring yourself so you can inspire everyone else. Overhead grows, there are more commas in all the numbers, and then environmental factors like supply chain woes, economic recessions, global pandemics, union strikes, and shipping variables throw the efforts of the business off course. One day you wake up and have that dreaded thought: "Why I am I even doing this?" Burnout is creeping in.

One useful antidote to burnout is to identify a clear sense of purpose. It's important to know what heading to be on and to orient your ship so that those winds can fill your sails. Having a personal "why" (or a list of "whys") is essential for reminding yourself of your purpose. It's also imperative that your business has a clearly defined purpose and that your team knows what that purpose is (and can repeat it when asked).

But how do you live in your purpose? You have to create margin in your life.

The most practical and tactical way to live daily in your purpose as an owner is to make your business more profitable. If your business has breathing room, then you can actually set out to accomplish your purpose. When you have margin then you can concern yourself with more than just making payroll. You can actually live your purpose out – and when you are living in your purpose, it changes your perspective on everything.

Profit Hiker exists to help you make your business more profitable so you can live in your purpose.

The Profit

Profit is the number one symptom of business health.

Just like we look at blood pressure to determine cardiac health or we measure oxygen levels in your blood to report lung health, we can look at profit as the leading metric of business health. There are plenty of other factors that play into a healthy business, such as the mission of the organization, how employees are treated, the social impact and so on – just like there are other factors that shine a light on your body's health, such as how much fiber you're eating or what your cholesterol levels are. But profit is the one key metric that you can take a quick look at and make a snap decision about the true health status of a business or organization, no matter the size.

Every organization needs breathing room to relieve pressure and open new doors. It doesn't matter if you're running a Fortune 100 company or a Boy Scout troop, you need to have a balanced budget with healthy margins that has breathing room at the end of each month and each year.

For some people, profit is a dirty word. You might even be embarrassed to admit that a business is profitable. It can become a taboo topic that's discussed behind closed doors. The word itself can conjure up images of industrialists dressed like the Monopoly man, twisting their mustaches while peering down on all of the common folk who are breaking their backs for him while he waits for his caviar to be served on fine china. Being concerned with profit does not make you a Big Bad Capitalist. Profit is absolutely necessary in order for you to achieve your purpose in business. Let that sink in: You cannot achieve your purpose in business if your business is not profitable. A business without profit is a hobby.

Profit isn't a good thing or a bad thing; it's just a thing. Just like money itself isn't good or bad, but can be used for good or bad, the same goes for profit in a business. Business owners have implemented abusive practices for millennia in the name of profit, but that does not mean that "profit" and "abuse" are necessarily correlated. It means that it's possible to use profit for abuse, just like it's possible to use profit to create a better workplace, or to leave a legacy for your children, or to invest in your community. It is what you make it to be.

Profit has *potential*.

Profit creates *possibilities*.

Profit fulfills *purpose*.

The Hike

Hiking is simply making a plan, preparing for a journey, and then putting one foot in front of the other until the journey is complete.

As an activity, hiking is full of eagerness, effort, and accomplishment. Hiking requires bravery and leads to adventure. Hiking supports health, blazes trails, makes memories, and forges character.

Do you know what it takes to be a hiker? All you have to do is start hiking! If you are hiking a flat, half-mile trail around a pond, you are a hiker. If you are climbing Mount Everest, you are a hiker. And when your hike is finished, aren't you always glad you did it?

One of my favorite hiking memories took place when I was 15 years old and my family went on a camping trip to the Grand Canyon. We had a hiking guide with a big group of several families, and every day we went on longer, prettier, more adventurous hikes deeper into the canyon. Every day there would be fewer and fewer people at the trailhead at meet-up time, and by the last day it was just a handful of us. My dad and I were the only representatives from our family, ready for the crescendo of the trip: hiking to the bottom and back up to the rim in the same day.

All the way down the trail, signs warned us not to do what we were doing. "WARNING: Do not attempt to hike to the bottom and back in the same day!" We took pictures with the signs for posterity's sake. There was certainly wisdom in those warnings, but we were with a guide who had done this many times before and assured us we were ready and able to do it.

It was a 17-mile round trip hike from where we were down to the Colorado River. On the way back up, the guide asked if we wanted to take a detour to Plateau Point, a scenic overlook. It would add several miles, but he assured us it would be worth it. When we got to the point, I recognized it from the postcards in the gift shop. It was one of those spectacular rock outcroppings that hangs out over the canyon. It was absolutely breathtaking to see in person. The experience of sitting out on that huge rock, surrounded by the magnitude and vastness of the canyon on all sides is powerfully memorable.

Of course, the whole way down the trail doubt crept in: Why are we doing this? Aren't we accomplishing enough just by going to the river and back up? What are we trying to prove to ourselves?

But that view was worth every single strained step and drop of sweat. After completing that hike, I wouldn't trade the memory of that accomplishment nor the excruciating effort it took to get there for anything.

That hike was one of the hardest physical experiences of my life. The last two or three miles up to the rim were absolutely brutal. It's some of the steepest parts of the trail, and we finished it in the dark. Heat still radiated off the rocks from being baked in triple digit heat all day. Now that I'm the age my dad was when he made that hike, I can hardly imagine tackling that with my boys – but it would be a worthwhile trip to make, even with all of the aches and pains from abuse on a middle-aged body trying to keep up with soon-to-be-teenagers.

Hiking can lead to incredible experiences, but the best experiences come from the greatest amount of effort. You get out what you put into a hike. That means the only thing stopping you from accomplishing greatness in your business is simply a plan and effort!

Hiking is *difficult*.

Hiking is *worth it*.

Hiking *takes you places* you've never imagined.

The Heart Behind Your Adventure

So why Profit Hiker?

If you've ever flown in a commercial airliner, you are familiar with the pre-flight safety instructions. They're the same for each of the more than 45,000 passenger flights per day in America.[1] Seatbelts, no smoking, floatation devices, exit doorways – you know the drill. What always stands out to me in the routine is the instruction for oxygen masks. As they say, "In the event of a change in cabin pressure" (or as comedian George Carlin quipped, "when the roof flies off"), an oxygen mask will appear from the compartment above you. The next instruction is key: put on your own mask before helping others. Why is that such an important instruction? Because we can't help anyone if we're suffocating.

Taking care of our own health is what gives us the ability to help others. This is especially true in business.

Healthy businesses can create tremendous leverage to radically change lives. From your customers to your employees, to yourself and your own family – even entire communities have been reclaimed, revived, and redeemed by a strong and thriving business.

One thing is for certain: a struggling business doesn't have that same leverage. Businesses that are sucking wind are filled with panic, fear, and anxiety. There is a looming sense of inescapable doom that makes thriving nearly impossible. Sound familiar? If you take care of yourself, then you'll be able to take care of everyone around you.

Profit is your oxygen mask.

Your *customers* need your business to be healthy.

If you want a healthy marriage, first, you need to treat your spouse well. Put their needs first, check in on them often, make sure you're going out on regular dates, and always be thinking how you can make their life better. By putting your spouse first, you create attraction. Selflessness is magnetic.

Customer relationships are the same way.

You want to grow your business? Put your customers first. If your business can focus on solving the problems of your customers, then it will thrive. Check in on them, make sure you are getting regular one-on-one face time, and always be thinking about how you can make their life better. This attitude is attractive.

But you can only focus on your customers when you no longer need to focus on yourself. If your business is constantly strapped for cash, just one hiccup away from going out of business, then it is very difficult to even have the capacity to care deeply about anyone else. Financial stress accounts for 37% of marriage divorces in the United States[2] which comes as no surprise for those who have experienced extreme financial stress themselves. When money pressure has been relieved, we are free both mentally and emotionally to turn our attention to others and invest more of ourselves into our relationships. This is as true in business as it is in marriage.

Profit is the doorway to deeper and stronger customer relationships, which directly correlates to long-term business growth.

Your *employees* need your business to be healthy.

Gig work, The Great Resignation, and "Quiet Quitting" become news bites that spread negativity when it comes to employment. Hating your job is a punchline in our culture – comic strips, sitcoms, and cinema all portray the same trope about a hollow soul having to drag themselves to work, dreaming about where they would rather be. It doesn't have to be this way.

According to a Gallup worldwide employment survey, nearly 60% of global workers are Quiet Quitting.[3] This term refers to mental disengagement from your work, which essentially comes from a lack of purpose. That same survey reports that "low engagement costs the global economy $8.8 trillion dollars, or 9% of global GDP."

Hiring is difficult these days, and we all know it. Getting talented people to work for you requires good pay, a great workplace environment, and work they can be proud of. Profit is the key to each and every one of these things.

Profit can build a place that people look forward to coming to each morning, to do fulfilling work, and leave satisfied at the end of the day. It takes money to pay competitively, to hire quality people, and to keep the team focused on the customers. It takes money to give back and to innovate. It takes money to buy better, faster, and safer equipment for your team to use.

This has an impact that carries beyond the four walls of the business, too. When employees have margin in their lives, their families flourish, and their overall satisfaction rises. Instead of working late at a job they hate and bringing their discouragement home, they can leave work at work, satisfied with a good day full of purposeful effort. This energy gets passed to their loved ones, multiplying your efforts.

Your team matters. Workplace satisfaction matters. People want to do good work that makes an impact.

Your *community* needs your business to be healthy.

When you build a healthy business, it gives you lots of options. One of these options is to give back into your community.

The United States is one of the most generous nations in the world both by total amount as well as per capita, but even so our annual giving averages just $1,204 per person.[4] From my experience in various communities, business owners are throwing the curve here. If there's a youth sports team that needs uniforms, small business owners step up to the plate. If a parade or fireworks show needs funding, small business owners sponsor the event. Non-profit fundraisers often feature both local sponsors, as well as the owners themselves showing generosity that goes above and beyond.

Small business owners often feel like the caretakers of their community. Your community needs you! But generosity is directly linked to profitability. You can only give from what you have. It is our responsibility as business owners to first make sure that our business is healthy so that we can give back. Remember the pre-flight oxygen mask instructions? If you don't take care of your business, not only are you unable to be helpful, but you also become a burden to those around you.

A Chick-fil-A franchise owner in Georgia pooled money from the team and bought one of his employees a new minivan. She is a single mom who was taking a taxi to work every day. He asked if she was having car trouble and learned that she didn't have a car at all. The team all pitched in, which was full of heart, but that alone wouldn't buy an entire new car. The business is what carried most of that financial burden. The owner had been responsible with the financial health of the business along with his own personal finances. This margin put him in the position to bless that woman in a huge way at just the right time.[5]

Whether you are investing your time as a board member or investing your money through sponsorships and charitable giving, the local community is relying on your business to continue to be healthy. If you have a generous heart, as many community business owners do, then it is your *responsibility* to make sure that your business is financially healthy and profitable so that you are always ready and able to be generous when the opportunity arises.

The same goes for your time. If you have a service business that does pro bono work, then your duty is to make sure you have margin in your billable hours. If your schedule is booked solid, then you couldn't donate your time even if you wanted to.

Community matters, and it is well worth the investment.

Your *relationships* need your business to be healthy.

Your friends and family can get the best of you when you're not chronically stressed about the health of your business. This doesn't end with profit, but it does begin with profit. Building margin in your business is the most useful lever you can pull in order to bring your best self into your relationships. Work stress can bleed into every close relationship you have, from your children to your spouse and your friends. I've been there: thinking about an unexpected cost while playing catch with my son or wondering what we're going to do after losing a huge client – instead of engaging in conversation with my wife or kids.

Relationships are what make our lives important. It's easy to say, but what we invest our time in shows what we really value. Your thoughts become decisions, which direct your actions. Over time your actions build a legacy. Every day we stack a single brick with our actions, and over time it becomes a monument to what we valued daily over the years. While the biggest splash you make in life may be at work, the deepest impact you can make is at home.

A strong sense of purpose, healthy boundaries, and a profitable business can set your personal relationships up for success. When your business is healthy, you have created an environment where you can be personally healthy as well – mind, body, and soul. In the words of author Jon Acuff, give your family "the best of you, not the rest of you."[6]

Relationships matter, and strong relationships become a deep part of who we are as people.

You need a healthy business.

Stress has holistic symptoms on your body and is a normal situational reaction – but we were not created to live in stress from wake to sleep. Your adrenal system releases adrenaline and cortisol into your bloodstream when triggered by stress. These combine into a cocktail that gives a football player the ability to beat a defender to the end zone for a game-winning touchdown. It's what gives a soldier the ability to fight at a high level for a long period of time, staying alert when they should be falling asleep. It's what helps you outrun that loose dog that you encountered on your morning jog. But our bodies are not designed to live with these hormones coursing through our veins all day, every day.

Cortisol puts your body into "fight-or-flight" mode. According to the Mayo Clinic, cortisol increases your blood sugar and helps your brain to use that sugar, along with giving resources to your muscle tissue for quick repair.[7] It also slows down your "non-essential" functions in a fight-or-flight scenario, such as your immune system, digestion, reproductive system, and parts of your brain that manage your mood and fear levels. Cortisol is really useful when you need it but is harmful when it is present all the time.

The real trouble with chronic stress is that if the stressor doesn't go away, our body begins to strain over time. Every major system in your body is affected by stress.[8] Cardiovascular, nervous, digestive, muscular, reproductive, and immune systems are impacted by chronic stress. It's no wonder that the average age of Americans is dropping every year!

It's a good thing there's hope for you as a business owner. Creating margin by finding better profit in your business can alleviate a lot of this stress. Of course, you will still have the typical challenges of a small business: trouble with suppliers, employees who go rogue, customer service, and changing competitive landscapes. But when you have a profitable business, you can invest in what gives you purpose, and it makes all of those hurdles a lot easier to face. The bonus is that your body will thank you.

You matter! As the leader of this mission, it is important that you take care of yourself so that you can accomplish the mission.

Define your own "Why"

This is your journey, so you need to know what your own "North Star" is. Why are you gearing up for a difficult trail? What's waiting for you at the top of that mountain? Is it for your family, your future, your community, your legacy, your employees, for yourself?

Take some time to really understand yourself here, because you will need your "Why" whenever the trail gets tough (and it will).

Are You Fit For The Journey?

What makes a Profit Hiker?

It is not easy to be a small business owner, and it is even more difficult to run a successful business. If you are looking for freedom and low stress, you won't find it in this arena. In fact, I never knew how easy I had it as an employee until I became an owner. A business owner's mind is always thinking about the business. When wondering "why am I even doing all of this?" I like to turn to the ancient wisdom.

Whether or not you know his story and his life, and regardless of your spiritual beliefs, it's agreed upon by most of the world that Jesus was a remarkable teacher. He spoke bluntly when needed, but most of the time he crafted his storytelling with outside-the-box perspectives woven with plenty of nuance. This was quintessential first-century Rabbi style – avoid a direct answer, rather, tell a story that creates space for curiosity and discussion. Thousands of years later, we are still discussing the true meaning behind his stories.

For example…

> *Enter through the narrow gate. For wide is the gate and broad is*
>
> *the road that leads to destruction, and many enter through it. But*
>
> *small is the gate and narrow the road that leads to life, and only a*
>
> *few find it (Matthew 7:13-14, NIV).*

Many people think that Jesus is speaking about eternity here, because he often did, but much more often he spoke to living in the present moment. I love reading an ancient text that contains humanity within it that is immediately relatable. It's amazing that with all of the changes in the world since then, this still rings true: we humans desire the path of least resistance. Water does too. So do wild animals. This mentality of seeking the easiest path is hard-wired into every aspect of our world. But the difficult path – the narrow road with the small gate – is the one worth striving for.

Profit Hikers take the hard path. It's the good way, but it's also the way that is stacked with obstacles, risk, and difficulty. Some will try and then give up to go right back to the broad path. But as a Profit Hiker, you must persist.

Characteristics of a Profit Hiker

CHARACTERISTIC #1: VISION

You need to blend imagination and wisdom together to envision a bright new future for your business. Some people are gifted as visionaries and don't need to work hard to see what the business could and should be. But a lot of us business owners are so buried in day-to-day tasks that it's hard to create space for imagination. If that sounds like you, there are some exercises (literally and figuratively) laid out at the end of this book that will help you create that space, because your business needs you to have Vision.

CHARACTERISTIC #2: BRAVERY

Synonyms of Bravery include valor, courage, and heroism. This word might spark images of soldiers charging the hill or first responders running straight into a tragedy, but you and I have opportunities to be brave every day. My favorite quote on the topic is from John Wayne: "Courage is being scared to death but saddling up anyway." I often remind my children that you don't have the opportunity for Bravery unless you're scared first. Bravery is not bravado – bravery is informed, while bravado is clueless. Difficult trails require Bravery.

CHARACTERISTIC #3: PLANNING

This is where the rubber meets the road. Bravery falls flat without a Plan. We will talk about a trail map, but that's not a Plan. A Plan involves more detail than just the map. If you have been on a hike, you know that a hiking plan involves what you're wearing, what the weather is expected to be, what time you depart, how much food to bring, how long should the breaks be, and how long should this hike take from start to finish. A Plan should also account for unforeseen adversity. Once you pick a trail, Plan out how you are going to go about that journey – and be realistic. You still have a business to run, not to mention all of your other responsibilities in life.

CHARACTERISTIC #4: COMMITMENT

Hiking requires a promise made and a promise kept from yourself to yourself. Once you decide to take this journey, there will be times when you will need to use your commitment as a binding contract to stay on course. That's how you should treat all promises made, but especially the hard ones that you've only made to yourself. If your Commitment is truly authentic, it will breed discipline. Accountability also helps. Share your Commitment with those you trust, and ask them to hold you to it.

CHARACTERISTIC #5: GRIT

Grit and commitment go together like peanut butter and jelly. Grit conjures up words like perseverance, unwavering, and firmness. It's that "no-quit" attitude that follows your commitment and fills you once you know your "why." Some people are naturally gritty. If that's you, then you're ready for the challenge. If you are not naturally gritty, then you need to become your own cheerleader. Find ways to remind yourself of why you are doing this, every single day. Use reminders on your phone, start each day with a prayer, or leave Post-it notes in high visibility places. Use whatever technique will help you stay motivated.

CHARACTERISTIC #6: HEART

Character, moxie, resolve – heart is the flip side of grit. If grit is what protects you from negativity, heart is the wellspring of positivity that keeps you going in tough times. Having heart means that you have hope. Purpose leads to vision, which creates hope, that in turn gives you the heart you need to finish the trail.

These are the characteristics of a Profit Hiker: Vision, Bravery, Planning, Commitment, Grit, and Heart. If you don't have all of these characteristics naturally, worry not – I don't think any one person has all of them. The good news is that you can practice and develop these characteristics. You can exercise any of these muscles.

Cross Training

Some time ago I lived on the coast and used to surf regularly. I was out by myself on one of those magical days where conditions line up perfectly. Rain was in the forecast, which keeps everyone at home. I thought it would be a fun, small surf morning and was willing to brave a little rain. It turned out to be fantastic surf, with perfectly shaped waves a little over head-high, pitching and peeling in a way that you see in magazines or video games. The rain was barely a drizzle, and I couldn't believe it.

The only problem was that I had picked the wrong board for the day. In surfing, you have to match the board to the size and style of the wave, and I had picked my biggest, slowest board: a 10-foot longboard. It's what surfers call a *log*: a slow, thick, wide board made for tiny summertime waves. But there was no way I was missing out on this surf. When it's good like that, it might change in an hour or two when the tide or wind shifts, and the surf could be gone. You have to work with what you have, and make it happen. So, I paddled out.

I caught a few waves and was pinching myself…nobody else was on the beach or in the water, and I was dropping into these fast, hollow waves. Nobody was going to believe me! It was on my third wave when I took off deep, getting a little too aggressive, and started to get barreled. It's only happened a few times in my life, when the wave is breaking overtop of you like a waterfall and you're tucked inside. It's a mind-blowing, high-fiving experience when that happens. But the board I was riding was too slow to keep up with the fast-breaking wave, and I was getting deeper and deeper. I got sucked into the "washing machine" which is when you get too deep in a hollow wave that's pitching out, and then flipped around and around like a rag doll. Normally I would have just taken my licks and paddled back out for more, except my big, slow board flipped up between my legs and jerked my lower leg to the side, right below my knee.

Immediately I felt that sharp, hot pain that tells you something went really wrong. It turns out I didn't tear anything, but it did stretch my medial collateral ligament into oblivion. It immediately became a dangerous situation: having a board that had broken loose and was somewhere between myself and the shore, unable to kick with my right leg, heavier-than-usual waves inbound, and absolutely nobody around. I was able to keep my head above water and was eventually able to swim to shore despite strong rip tides, but I could barely stand up under my own power. It took a long time to drag that big, heavy board up the beach, but I was able to get back to the truck eventually.

The doctor informed me that the stronger I could make my quadriceps, the faster my knee would stabilize and heal. The only outdoor activity left for me to do was ride a bike, so I took to it every day. I would get off work, change clothes, and hit the road trying to get stronger legs so I could get back in the water. I even lowered my seat a little bit so that my quads would burn more. I pushed myself to the point of sucking wind every single day, making my legs stronger.

What I didn't know was that I was also making my mind stronger.

When it came time to get back in the water, I took the mental fortitude I had forged on two wheels into the surf with me. Surfing can be a really challenging activity, literally battling forces of nature in a quest to dance with Mother Ocean. The sea can break your spirit in an instant. What I hadn't realized until this point was that I had been surfing with a weak mental attitude for years. There are some days when the ocean feasts upon the timid, and it takes Grit to push through and tame the waves. Looking back, there were clearly two different chapters of my surfing journey: pre-knee and post-knee.

I had practiced Grit while mountain biking and carried that characteristic into surfing. Even today, I am still able to tap into that "muscle memory" of Grit when needed. You can do the same thing for your journey with your business. What activities can you do to sharpen your Vision, Bravery, Planning, Commitment, Grit, and Heart?

This is what it takes to build the characteristics of a Profit Hiker. Next, we'll dig into the trails themselves.

The Trails To Take

There are 11 trails you can take to gain elevation and a healthier, more profitable business. We are going to explore each one in the following format:

Trail Rating

LENGTH

All trails vary in length. The ratings for our trails are going to be Scenic Loop, Day Hike, and Backpacking Trip. The length of the trail determines how prepared you need to be.

DIFFICULTY

Trails also vary in difficulty and are each a fit for varying levels of expertise. In the hiking world, you have Class 1 through Class 5 hikes. Class 5 trails are rock-climbing, cliffhanging, death-defying hikes. Profit Hiker isn't about life-or-death situations, so we are going to stick to Class 1, 2 and 3 hikes, ranging from easy to difficult in that order. Class 3 trails are for more experienced hikers.

ELEVATION GAIN

This is the big payoff! Find out what the upside of each hike is. The ratings are Foothill, Alpine, and Summit. Foothill hikes can be easy wins, Alpine hikes are very rewarding, but Summit hikes will radically change your life.

The Overlook

We'll take a high-level look at each trail, so you know what you're in for before hiking it.

The Routes

Each trail has several routes. In hiking, there are often side trails, spurs, shortcuts, and scenic routes. Sometimes it's worth staying on the beaten path, but often it's worth a little extra work to take another route.

Around The Campfire

With each of these trails, we explore real-life stories of businesses that took the trail and gained elevation.

Caution Signs

Beware of danger that might be lying ahead on each trail.

Preparation

Before hiking each trail, you should ask yourself some questions to make sure it's the right trail for your business at this time.

The Trailhead

This is where the hike begins. You will have a clear next step to take on this particular trail.

Your Sherpa

No matter what trail you are hiking, it's good to have wise counsel, a helpful guide, someone who knows the trail inside and out, and perhaps can even help carry your burden. Each trail has a recommended relationship to take with you on the journey.

Trail Markers

When you're on the trail, it's encouraging to see a trail marker from time to time. A simple arrow fixed to a tree can encourage you that you're heading in the right direction. There will be metrics in your business that indicate if you're on the trail or have strayed off of it and need to make a course correction.

For the sake of clarity, we are going to use the following terms interchangeably:

- Brand
- Business
- Small Business
- Organization
- You

And we will be interchanging these terms as well:

- Customers
- Clients
- Audience

Profit Hiker is a program that you can apply to a local boutique or a global conglomerate, so insert yourself into the story here. If you are running a small business, a digital side hustle, a well-known brand or you're trying to take your Parent Teacher Association to the next level, there will be at least one trail for you to take.

Now let's explore the trails...

Raise Prices

LENGTH: SCENIC LOOP

DIFFICULTY: CLASS 1

ELEVATION GAIN: ALPINE

The Overlook

You can make your business more profitable without growing! While most small business owners immediately turn to sales and marketing, typically the lowest hanging fruit for profitability is going to be on your operations side.

If your audience knows you, loves you, and trusts you then you can probably raise your prices right now. Raising prices is all about expectations and value. If the perceived value that the shopper is expecting from you meets or exceeds the price of the product or service, then they will consider purchasing it. In the words of Warren Buffet–one of the most successful investors of all time– "Price is what you pay. Value is what you get." [9]

Amidst inflation and higher cost of fuel (not to mention building materials like steel and lumber), everyone is expecting prices to raise on everything. If you haven't raised your prices in a while, your time to do that may be right now.

The Routes

RAISE PRICES FOR NEW CLIENTS

If you have a service, you can raise prices right now for new clients. New clients won't know—and don't need to know—what rates your existing clients are paying. You can always keep a discount in your back pocket if you feel like you're going to lose a sale over it. It's a lot easier to give a discount when your prices have already raised!

RAISE PRICES ON EVERYTHING, ALL AT ONCE

If you have a product, then you can raise your prices right now. Just declare it so. It may be quite a chore if you have tons of product variations and a Point Of Sale (POS) system that you run everything through, so you may need to dedicate some serious time to the project, but think about what a difference it will make when it's done.

Around The Campfire

STEEL TRAP

I once helped a company that sells pre-engineered buildings grow their brand in a commodity market, allowing them to raise their prices. When it comes right down to it, metal buildings are metal buildings. They all use the same materials, often from the same exact suppliers; they are designed pretty much the same. This company had done a fantastic job of creating a sales engine that ran like a Swiss watch. They just needed to bring their marketing into the digital age.

We helped them craft some compelling messaging and a visual ecosystem that explained the features and benefits of their products in a way that their competition simply wasn't doing. This justified a price increase above their competition. Combine that with the on-phone experience that customers received once they had decided to take the next step, and you have a brand that is growing despite selling the exact same product as the other folks.

OVERHEAD OVATION

When I merged my service business with another one, my new business partner approached me with a plan to raise prices on my clients to get them up to speed with the rest of the clients. I had been a self-employed, solo practitioner working out of my spare bedroom and had nearly zero overhead. But now I had an office with employees and everything that comes with that – a legion of computer hardware, desks, printers, on and on and on. But I also had a new world of services to offer, and much more bandwidth. In other words, I had created a lot of value for my clients overnight. On paper, it's an easy choice, but it can be difficult to actually reach out to someone and let them know that I am now expensive. In this case, I was raising prices by over 50%, and I was really concerned about losing customers, or at least making them upset. I had been their trusted advisor, walking side-by-side with them in their business growth, but I knew it was time. It was a simple decision, but it turns out it was difficult to actually take that trail. In the end, I didn't lose one client with the price raise. The strong relationships I had built really helped us kick off our business together.

DOLLAR AND CHANGE

Dollar Tree, the dollar store famous for everything being $1 no matter what, amidst rapid inflation raised their prices to $1.25. They raised their prices by 25% overnight, and their price was literally in the brand name! It made news headlines, but the stores are still full of shoppers. Even at the new price, they continue to provide good value and grow.[10]

Caution Signs

If you are in a commodity war, then raising prices might be a death sentence without clearly adding value. You absolutely have to be aware of what your competition has to offer and how far you can push your customers before they jump ship and go for the cheaper option.

One antidote to a commodity war is a strong brand. Investing in your brand, and helping people connect with something bigger than just the product itself, is a way to opt out of a commodity war.

Another antidote is an extremely high level of service. Responsiveness, customer service, friendliness and consistently delivering promises can provide enough value to justify a higher cost for the exact same product. I have experienced this in my own business journey. I have won business time after time in a commodity market simply by answering the phone and being as helpful as I can, while my competitors screen their calls with voicemail.

Preparation

What is everyone else charging?

Should I match competitive pricing?

Am I providing more value than I am charging for?

The Trailhead

Start with your products and services. If you don't have a clear menu of your offerings, now is the time to make one.

Your Sherpa

ACCOUNTANT

Your accountant might be able to weigh in here. Accountants get a look behind the curtain of all kinds of small businesses and can usually tell you right off the bat where you stand in the competitive landscape. This is especially true if you have a seasoned accountant who has a large firm and lots of clients. They can really have their finger on the pulse of the business community, what businesses are financially healthy, and what you should be charging.

Trail Markers

The top line revenue on your Profit and Loss statement will show your progress. This should be going up over time. If nothing else in your business changes, you should become more profitable.

Reduce Costs

LENGTH: SCENIC LOOP

DIFFICULTY: CLASS 2

ELEVATION GAIN: FOOTHILL

The Overlook

"There's gold in them there *BILLS*!" We're mining for profit that might be lying dormant all around you. Reducing your costs is a reliable trail towards better profit. When taking this trail, you should look at *all* of your costs, and start with the largest first. Typically, this will be a building lease, your team, or Cost of Goods Sold, depending on the type of business you have. For many small businesses, these will be the top three cost centers. You're not going to slash those expenses out, but you might have more wiggle room than you think. Saving a small percentage of a big expense is worth more than trying to save on a bunch of small expenses – so focus on the primary ones first and foremost.

Step one: find competing bids for your suppliers. This process has several benefits. First, you'll see where you're at in the market, and how much opportunity there is to improve. You may have had it good already, but you won't know until you shop around. Second, it's often best to have more horses in the stable, and it's wise to be aware of what supplier options there are for you. And finally, you can gain some leverage for the conversations you'll have with your existing suppliers, if you think there's room to improve your costs.

Then you'll want to approach your current and most expensive third-party suppliers. Honesty is the best policy in this process; let them know that you've shopped around, but that you've appreciated working with them (if that is the case). Make sure they know that you want to continue this partnership for a long time, and simply ask if there is anything they can do with the price. This assumes that you have a healthy relationship with them, which I believe is always a good way to do business. Kindness can be practical when you need it to be. If you have a contentious relationship with your landlord or suppliers, then you will probably need to seek competitive bids before trying to negotiate. You only have leverage in that relationship when you have the ability (and maybe even the desire) to walk away. You'll find out how important to them you really are.

If your lease is up in the next six to twelve months, it's time to shop around. Typically, it's better for everybody if you can stay in your location unless you've outgrown it, but you need to know how the market stands. You also need plenty of time for negotiation. Finding middle ground on a lease renewal can be a slow process, and time is on your landlord's side, not yours. Make sure you know well in advance what the going rate is for your type of space. Generally, you're going to compare the "dollar per square-foot per month" rate. You also need to know whether that rate includes "Net Net Net" (also known as "Triple Net" or "NNN"), which means you pay for all expenses of the building as well, including property taxes, insurance, utilities, and sometimes even maintenance. If your business has been trending down lately either from market conditions or personal struggles, be honest with your landlord. I have worked with several small businesses who have opened their books for their landlord and asked what can be done. If you pay on time and are a good tenant for a long time, they often see tremendous value in keeping you around and will work with you to get through your downturn. Sometimes they might forgive a few months and amend the lease to add those months onto the back end.

As far as your employees go, you should tread lightly. Once you pay someone a certain amount, it's hard to un-ring that bell. The expectation is set, and you can't go back down without damaging the relationship. What you can control is the salaries of your new hires, so make sure that you're hiring right and not overspending. That doesn't mean hire cheap, especially in an environment where good people are in high demand; it simply means to hire at the right price and not over.

After taking a close look at your business, you may find that you have an employee who's not pulling their weight, and you'll have to deal with that one way or another. But it's better to discover that as soon as possible in order to either reduce costs or increase productivity in that role.

Another way to reduce your costs, at least from a cashflow perspective, is to refinance your business debt. This is not for everyone. If you have a loan that's been paid down a few years but still has no end in sight, you should consider refinancing that loan into the same total length you are currently in. For instance, if you have a 10-year loan that you are three or four years into, you can potentially refinance that loan back into a 10-year with a lower total amount. You have earned equity by paying the current loan down, so your monthly payments should be a lot less. The downsides to this technique are that you will have to repay loan origination fees, and it may not even work out at all if interest rates are much higher than before. But if current interest rates are the same or less than the loan you have now, take a close look at refinancing.

Finally, the easiest part of this trail (with the smallest reward) is simply going through your previous month's expenses and deciding what to cut out. Be honest about what the business actually needs – sometimes free coffee and snacks for employees is a nice morale booster, but other times employees can become ungrateful and entitled about these little benefits. Those small expenses can quickly add up to thousands of dollars per year. If those smaller expenses are bringing real value to the business, even if you can't measure it in dollars, then you may want to keep them.

Controlling your costs is an action that you can take one time to continue to pay dividends into the future.

The Routes

SLASH EXPENSES

The simplest way to navigate this trail is to go through your books and trim the fat. You don't need to be a financial expert. Just take a look at your most recent bank statement and question everything.

NEGOTIATE WITH VENDORS

This can be a delicate conversation, so tread lightly when needed. The bottom line: if you and your suppliers both need each other, then you can come up with a new win-win scenario.

FIND NEW SUPPLIERS

It almost never hurts to explore what other options may be available. Depending on your industry, there may be new options or innovations since you last checked.

RE-NEGOTIATE YOUR LEASE

If you have a good relationship with your landlord, it may be worth the conversation. It also depends on the business climate and how in-demand commercial space is in your area.

REFINANCE YOUR DEBT

If you have a business loan that is partially paid down, refinancing it to the original term will almost certainly bring your monthly payment down, helping with cashflow and margin.

Around The Campfire

DELTA CHANGES

In 2018, Delta Airlines made one simple change to their business that saved millions of dollars per year. As you can imagine, the cost of jet fuel is one of the biggest drivers in an airline's ability to make money. Someone in the organization took a creative approach to reducing costs by reducing weight. One of the decisions was to reduce the weight of the in-flight magazine by 1 ounce by printing on lighter paper, resulting in 11 pounds of weight savings on a Boeing 737 plane. This may not sound like much, but with thousands of flights per day and over a million per year, it quickly adds up. According to their calculations, this one simple change now saves 170,000 gallons of fuel every year, which results in hundreds of thousands of dollars to the bottom line.[11]

DON'T DOUBT THE DEBIT

I had a business partner who would control costs once or twice a year by cancelling the company debit card. It's a handy technique for a small business owner who often doesn't have the bandwidth to pick through your Profit and Loss statement and control every expense. It flips this trail on its head and puts you in charge of controlling expenses. The vendors will come knocking on your door to get paid, which opens the conversation about how much you're paying compared to the value you're getting.

Caution Signs

You should be wary of a human psychological response called "Loss Aversion." A 1979 study titled "Prospect Theory: An Analysis of Decision under Risk" is credited by Columbia University as "the most cited paper in economics and is among the most cited in psychological science" and singularly defined how Loss Aversion affects people.[12] To put it simply: most people feel more strongly about losing $100 than they do about gaining $100. Keep this in mind when cutting costs, and tread lightly.

Preparation

What other suppliers am I not currently using, but perhaps should?

Do I know what suppliers my competitors are using?

What level of expenses are normal for my industry?

Where can I trim my operations without reducing perceived value?

The Trailhead

Take a good look at your financials, starting with either your Profit and Loss statement or last month's bank statement. Working with your bookkeeper can help.

Your Sherpas

ACCOUNTANT

If you have a good small business accountant, then they are comfortable with financials of a business your size and can give you good insight to what your costs should be.

PROCUREMENT CONSULTANT

There are specialized advisors who negotiate with vendors on your behalf. If you do a lot of shipping or have accounts with massive companies, this person can save you quite a bit of time and money.

Trail Markers

Your Cost of Goods Sold and/or Expenses should be going down over time. If your sales stay consistent while this happens, you will be more profitable.

Turn Overhead Into A Profit Center

LENGTH: BACKPACKING TRIP

DIFFICULTY: CLASS 3

ELEVATION GAIN: ALPINE

The Overlook

This trail requires a creative look at your organization. It's easy to fall into a routine and a specific identity with your business. Over time, what you do can become who you think you are. Being stuck in a rut isn't necessarily a bad thing, in fact it often means that you're on a well-worn path and you're heading places. But it just might be the same path that everyone else is taking as well, and you could be missing out on some fantastic new trails.

The truth is that there are probably several hidden ways that you can create a new revenue stream in your business without hardly changing anything. The goal of this trail is to take any notable expenses and leverage those for other people.

Here is how you should think about it in its simplest form: on your Profit and Loss statement, is there a cost or category in "Expenses" that can also be "Income"? Or, if you are looking at your Balance Sheet, is there something that is under "Liabilities" that could really become "Assets"?

For a small business, the place to start is to think about the things that you do for free. If you offer a consultation or free quote, consider charging something for it. That accomplishes several goals at once: you capture revenue, establish value right away, and weed out the "tire kicker" shoppers who won't end up being customers anyhow (or at least won't become good customers).

You can also look at every single expense in your business as a possible asset. Your office or warehouse space, your fleet, your team, your equipment, your inventory, and even your supplies can be leveraged to capture surprise revenue.

The Routes

USE YOUR INVENTORY

Survey what products you stock and how else they might be leveraged for your business. Depending on how well you track inventory, you may have some unexpected extra stock.

USE YOUR EMPLOYEES

If your team has down time, that can be used either to help your current business or dream up a new way for them to be useful.

USE YOUR EQUIPMENT

If you have equipment that is sitting unused for periods of time, you could possibly rent it out to others. It could be as small and simple as a copy machine or as big as a crane.

USE YOUR SPACE

The more rare, expensive, and difficult your space is to get into, the more valuable it is to others. If you have commercial equipment or special permitting available, then you might be able to rent out your space during off-hours.

USE YOUR CUSTOMERS

Depending on who your customers are, they might be highly valuable to other people. There may be a partnership, advertising, or lead generation opportunity right inside your book of business.

Around The Campfire

CHICKEN CHANGE

The $4.99 rotisserie chicken at Costco is legendary. It is a wildly popular dinner-in-a-box that makes for a quick, hot meal. The chicken had been a loss leader for years, and Costco was fine losing 50 cents a bird just to get foot traffic that they couldn't get otherwise. It is brilliantly placed at the back of the store, requiring that you have to walk past a hundred yards of irresistible merchandise to get it. Costco knew that if they could get you in the door, that you would buy more than just the chicken. In fact, shoppers would commonly walk in to buy a chicken and walk out with a cart full of hundreds of dollars of merchandise.

Despite this brilliantly simple loss leader technique, it was time for a change. A few years ago, they decided to not lose money on the chicken anymore and invested in the chicken supply chain throughout the Midwest. They built and financed untold numbers of gigantic buildings for farmers, developed the meat packing systems, and knocked a whole dollar off of their cost. This effort resulted in a $90 million bump to the bottom line! What an incredible way to turn a loss into a win.

STARTING WITH A SPARK

Ford Motor Company has a reputation for disruptive innovation unlike any other company in modern American history. A lesser-known tangent of Henry Ford's legacy is another brand you'll find in American homes from coast to coast: Kingsford Charcoal.

Early "motor coaches" were primarily made of wood, and as part of his expansion plan, Ford set out to vertically integrate his wood supply chain. This involved huge swaths of forest land, sawmill operations, and chemical treatment facilities. A massive byproduct of a sawmill is wood chips. Ford saw an opportunity to "waste not," and his team developed a method for turning those chips into fuel. They would be dried, baked, mixed with starch, and pressed into bricks for portability.[13] They were used in Ford operations, but the volume was huge, and the commercial opportunity became evident in the coming years, first with restaurants and eventually in retail stores. So, Henry Ford, being himself, set out to create an entirely different business that is now nearly as well-known as his cars.

PANDEMIC PIVOTS

For all its ups and downs, 2020 was a lightning bolt of creativity, waking us from our sleepy routines. This moment in time launched small businesses everywhere from the status quo to an "innovate or die" mentality. In my town, local bars farmed out their employees for lawn care and trashcan cleaning, just to keep them employed. Restaurants sold raw materials, like flour and toilet paper that their customers couldn't find on the shelves at grocery stores. I remember reading one story about a commercial toilet paper manufacturing plant that opened up a retail drive through. Restaurants that held their pride in their fine dining experience and high level of service turned into drive-throughs in order to continue serving their customers and helping to keep their suppliers in business.

⚠️

Caution Signs

Once you have identified a way to turn overhead costs into a profit center, be careful not to let it consume you. As they say, "dance with the one that brought you" – don't ignore the main part of your business. Let this be what it is: a side project. New ideas and initiatives can often bring you renewed energy as a business owner. When there is a new playing field, you may be itching to explore it. But this, like every other exercise in Profit Hiker, should be one more small trail you take to hike a little further up the mountain.

Preparation

What assets does my business have, such as vehicles or equipment?

Does my team have any down time?

What can my space offer? (For instance, do I have a commercial kitchen with proper health permits or a usable space outdoors?)

Do I have a big enough audience to sell advertising?

Am I turning away business? Can I sell those contacts as sales leads to other businesses?

The Trailhead

Dive into your financials and make a short list of your biggest expenses.

Your Sherpa

BUSINESS CONSULTANT

An outside perspective can be helpful in this process because sometimes we tend to be too close to our business to think creatively about our assets and resources.

Trail Markers

Cost centers will become profit centers on your Profit and Loss report and your Balance Sheet.

Optimize

LENGTH: DAY HIKE

DIFFICULTY: CLASS 2

ELEVATION GAIN: ALPINE

The Overlook

Your business likely has many opportunities to streamline systems, tasks, environments, and processes. Optimization is simply that.

If you think about your business like a freeway, some sections have five lanes with long straightaways, where people don't have to navigate obstacles or spend mental energy on defensive driving. They can simply put the pedal to the metal, stay in their lane, and go. But if your business is like every other business that's ever existed, you also have on-ramps and off-ramps, mergers, and some lane closures that cause traffic slowdowns. If you have the same tendencies that I do, you probably also have checkpoints to perform manual inspections, completely slowing the flow of traffic to a crawl. Don't let this happen to your business! As the Chief Freeway Designer, it's your job to make sure traffic is as smooth as can be, everywhere and all the time.

Begin by thinking about who is most valuable to the operation of your business. If that person had an extra hour a day, what would they do with it? How would that change the future of your business? Then, it's time to take a very close look at what everyone is doing every day. Take note of what tasks they perform, especially the repetitive and redundant tasks. Explore how you can remove those redundancies.

Optimization can be as simple or complex as you desire. You might be able to improve workflow, efficiency, and morale by simply rearranging your workspace. Better light, more elbow room, easier access, quicker to get from here to there – these are all optimizations.

Optimization can also be building better insights into the data of your business, so you can make better (and faster) decisions. Data is modern-day currency. You should be thinking how information and insights will inform your business choices.

The Routes

OBSERVE AND REPORT

Watch your business work as a curious outsider without emotional involvement. Identify friction points at every level of operation, document them well, and address the team with observations.

CREATE NEW SYSTEMS

A system is anything that creates repeatable improvement. In your business, a new system could be an investment into time management or project management software for your team. Or a new system might simply be printing out invoices, so you don't forget to pay them on time.

INVEST IN INSIGHTS

Every business has blind spots. More than likely, essential data is hiding somewhere in your business that would change your decision-making if you could see it in real time. Building a "dashboard" or "command center" can be a pivotal improvement.

Around The Campfire

THE TRANSPARENT DASHBOARD

One of my business partners has a fantastic mind for operations and set up a Project Management System that pretty much ran our entire business. System reports gave us valuable insight into what the team was working on, what our pipeline of work looked like, and what the future held for the business. Gantt charts, pie charts, and other visual data displays helped the management team make important decisions. The system had a dashboard to immediately diagnose and triage potential problems lying ahead, such as low sales or overloaded fulfillment.

DUST TO THRUST

I once had a team of very talented graphic designers that produced fantastic work at an impressive pace. One up-and-coming star designer was having difficulty with his computer. It was slowing him down, which was costing us real money. It was an older machine, likely the oldest and slowest on the team, maybe even in the entire office. I've done a few computer repairs in the past, so, together, we took it apart and cleaned off the heat sink, motherboard, fan, and air ducts. This took a little less than an hour, and it was up and running again. It was also a good teaching moment to help him diagnose and fix a computer problem, but the best thing to do in that scenario would be to simply get a new computer. While thousands of dollars in capital expense wasn't realistic at that moment in time, a lease would have been an easy decision. In this day and age, it does not make business sense to allow a slow computer to slow down your talented team – especially if they are part of your actual production.

⚠️

Caution Signs

Don't remove the humanity from this process. Your team is your talent, and they are not robots. Lean on the people who do the work you're looking to optimize, because they will be your best insight into where every friction point is. Do this by asking them questions about what frustrations they have, what opportunities they see, and what ideas they have to make things better. Stay humble, don't make assumptions, be curious, embrace empathy, and you'll be surprised at what you find.

Preparation

What person or role has become a bottleneck in my organization?

What tasks are holding my team back?

What tools are slowing us down?

Where can I remove friction in our operations?

The Trailhead

Observe your operations and look for areas of friction. Depending on how many moving parts you have in your business, this might take a day, or it might take a month. Then identify areas where a simple and repeatable improvement would make a big impact. Prioritize the pinch points and tackle improvements one by one.

Your Sherpa

BUSINESS CONSULTANT

Outside advice is usually helpful here, because you get so close to the day-to-day facets of your business that it becomes difficult to see opportunities for change.

Trail Markers

Your products and services should begin to be delivered faster or with fewer resources. Your business reports should become more robust and insightful.

Automate

LENGTH: DAY HIKE

DIFFICULTY: CLASS 2

ELEVATION GAIN: ALPINE

The Overlook

Automation is a spinoff of Optimization, but it deserves its own trail. Automation is essentially building a system that does what people used to do, typically with software or hardware (such as robotics).

As people become more expensive and difficult to keep on staff, it makes more and more sense to invest time, energy, and money into automations. Investing in systems is a longer-term payoff relative to some of these other trails, but it can be a fantastic investment into your business. Think about the relief your team would feel if you built a system that replaced the most repetitive processes or boring tasks. The immediate payoff is in boosted morale, both from your team and yourself. The long-term payoff is in profit.

Automation can be as simple as recording your onboarding training so that you (or key employees) don't have to burn time training a new team member.

If you don't have a Customer Relationship Management (CRM) system, this might be the easiest game-changing automation you can make in your business. A CRM system simplifies your interactions with potential and existing customers, and will completely change the way your sales and support staff operate.

Automation can also be an investment in new software or equipment that works better, faster, or more reliably. There could be an improvement to the efficiency of your operations that's yearning to be made, but you might instead be trying to ride it out with slow, outdated, or broken infrastructure.

Artificial Intelligence (AI) is really making waves in business automations, and it might be a fit for you too. Small business owners have been using AI chat tools such as ChatGPT to generate ideas, identify patterns, or get answers to difficult questions. Investing in an AI integration into your business can pay off huge, especially when it comes to customer service. This is a quickly evolving sector, and we should see some pretty neat automation tools coming into the market very soon.

The Routes

INVEST IN A "CRM"

"Customer Relationship Management" (CRM) software can change the game for your sales and customer service teams. It puts all of your customers and leads in one place, creates transparency for management, and has reporting built right in.

RECORD YOUR TRAINING

Training videos aren't just for huge corporations. If you have trained more than one person with the exact same information, then you should be recording this training and having them watch it before sitting down one-on-one.

NEW HARDWARE AND SOFTWARE

Depending on what type of business you're in, your equipment or your software tools might be holding your team back. Ask your team and find out how they are being limited. Then prioritize the improvements and create space in your budget.

In addition to transparency and accountability, a Project Management System can bring automation to your team as well. You can templatize processes, set up checkpoint notifications, and create repeatable tasks that relieve your team of redundant work.

ROBOTICS AND ARTIFICIAL INTELLIGENCE

You can also integrate robotic systems and Artificial Intelligence (AI) into your business to relieve pressure and dangerous tasks from your team members.

Around The Campfire

CHICKEN COOPS TAKE FLIGHT

One of the businesses that I own sells chicken coops. You can design and order a walk-in chicken coop from four to sixty feet long, and it gets delivered directly to you. Due to the built-to-order nature of the product, my processes were manual, very clunky, and had lots of opportunities to fail. If a customer asked about their order status, I had to dig and dig in order to find it. I had virtually no sales process, with a basic text file full of random notes, names and numbers cobbled together in cryptic messages that I couldn't even interpret sometimes. Without a good system, I had made it really difficult for people to buy my products. Looking back, it was just plain difficult to run the business in general.

I brought a partner into this business, and it was the best decision for removing all of these hurdles, hiccups, and headaches. He immediately fired up a Customer Relationship Management (CRM) system, and together we built a Project Management System just like we had with other businesses we owned.

A CRM was a game changer for my chicken coop business, but so was streamlined Project Management. Once we had the project process built out, we had a "command center" style dashboard that showed every single sale, where we're at in the process, and a snapshot for the entire operations side of the business in one quick glance. It's simply amazing. It's also totally transparent – anybody who needs to know what's going on can check in on it and have the same information that used to be either in a paper notepad or some files on my computer.

Those two systems took one month of hard work to set up in the off-season of the business and have now been paying off dividends for years. That is the real power in optimization and automation investments: they start paying back on day one and continue paying into the future.

STREAMLINED SCREENCASTS

Another great example of automation in my personal businesses was shared with me when I sold a business. I was to train the new owner on my operations, and also provide materials so that he could effectively train others in the future. I started planning an in-person session when he asked me to simply screencast it and save the videos. I was blown away by this simple idea – I had been sitting down one-on-one with our employees and training them the same way for seven years, and it had never once occurred to me to record one single session to save time and effort down the road. We are talking about hundreds of hours of opportunity cost – in a word, "margin" – completely wasted because I simply never thought of it. These days, you can bet that I take this repeatable, scalable mentality into every single training session I create.

⚠️

Caution Signs

Once again, don't turn your back on humanity while hiking this trail. Treat automation as a way to bless your employees with more bandwidth, not to replace them with AI. If you can remove the robot-like tasks from your team, they will be given the freedom to flourish as only humans can: with creativity and "organic" intelligence.

📖

Preparation

What repetitive tasks do I find myself and my key team members doing every day?

Can these tasks be completed by using machinery or equipment?

Can these tasks be completed with software automations?

Which of these tasks can be completed by an assistant (human or otherwise)?

The Trailhead

Observe your operations and look for repetition. You really need to view your business as an unemotional, objective outside observer. Once you have a list of repetitive tasks, triage that list into what can be accomplished with software and what can be accomplished with hardware. Then start with software and begin implementing improvements.

Your Sherpa

BUSINESS CONSULTANT

Once again, outside advice can help you discover opportunities that may be obvious in hindsight, but that you may be right now.

➡️

Trail Markers

Your products and services should begin to be delivered faster or with fewer resources.

The Same Product For More Of The Same Audience

LENGTH: SCENIC LOOP

DIFFICULTY: CLASS 1

ELEVATION GAIN: FOOTHILL

The Overlook

Marketing is where most small business owners turn when they want to grow and yield better profit. You want more leads, more customers, and more revenue. You pay to play, and if you do it right then you see a return on the investment. This area of growth is equal parts art and science. Data will help you gain insights for planning, evaluating, and reacting. But at the end of the day, you need to know your audience inside and out, and be able to speak to their desires. That's where the art comes into play: saying the right things to the right people at the right time. In the words of business guru Donald Miller, "If you want to sell more products there are only two ways to do it: sharpen up your marketing, or get more leads."[14]

When you're launching a new marketing campaign, this trail splits at the trailhead. There are actually two paths that have different end goals, but both of them get you up the mountain. You need to choose between a Direct Response campaign and a Branding campaign.

Direct Response campaigns are about accomplishing a specific goal within a certain amount of time in order to gain a Return On Investment (ROI). The best performing Direct Response campaigns have an offer and a deadline. There may be a sale for a limited time, an event on a certain date, or a coupon that expires. These campaigns leverage urgency and "fear of missing out" to encourage action. Ideally, you would be able to track your sales starting from dollars spent on ads all the way to net profit.

Branding campaigns are about awareness and are a very slow burn. This trail will be flat for a long time, and you just need to keep putting one foot in front of the other until you start to see an incline. On average, it takes seven ad impressions before a viewer will acknowledge your brand.[15] For most small businesses, Branding campaigns are something to grow into once you have a Direct Response system that works well. It's a long-term investment in your business that pays a return in years, not months or weeks.

Be sure to spend the right amount on advertising. You could be spending too much or too little, and there's not an exact amount. Budgeting five to ten percent of your total expenses is common, but if you have a strong reputation that creates lots of referrals, you may not need to advertise as much. If you're brand new, you will need to advertise more.

"Targeting" is when you choose exactly who your audience should be. Overspending might be disguised as Targeting. If you are targeting too broadly, then you are most certainly wasting ad impressions. If you are targeting too tightly, then you might be overpaying when you look at your cost per lead.

Since there is a scientific aspect to marketing, you need to continually experiment. This begins with your ad messaging. You may have an idea of what you think will resonate with your audience, but you don't know until you try. Try an "A/B" test where you run two different ads at the same time and see which performs best.

Do people know what you are asking them to do? In marketing this is your "Call To Action" (CTA) and it should be clear and easy. For example, if you advertise on the radio, then directing listeners to a memorable web address is easier to remember than a phone number.

If you hit a home run with your marketing campaign, be ready to service your new leads. Make sure you have a CRM and the manpower to actually connect people with your business once they show interest.

You cannot determine whether a campaign is successful unless you know what you would pay per lead. Real estate agents pay thousands of dollars in commission to a buyer's agent for a lead if the sale goes through. Every industry is different. If you don't know where to start, just begin with one dollar. Would you pay one dollar to get a chance to sell your product or service to someone? What about a thousand dollars? A hundred? Ten? Keep bracketing down the high and low numbers until you are comfortable with the price range. This is now your official Cost Per Lead (CPL).

Then, if you know your average close rate (percentage of leads that become sales), you can divide your CPL by your close rate percentage to calculate your Customer Acquisition Cost (CAC).

Divide your average sale price by your CAC and then you can report Return On Ad Spend (ROAS).

If you know your average customer Lifetime Value (LTV), or how much they will spend with you after all of their future repeat purchases, then you can report your cost of new revenue.

Combine that with your profit margin, and you now have your ROI for actual profit, dollar-to-dollar.

Very few small businesses are set up to report each link in this chain, but if you can, then you will have a winner.

The Routes

GET BETTER AT TARGETING

Make sure your marketing is targeted – are you reaching the right people? Who are they? In marketing it's called your customer "archetype" or "avatar." It can be helpful to give them a real-life name and describe their daily life, such as occupation, hobbies, and relationships.

IMPROVE YOUR FUNNEL

Imagine a funnel that you would use to fill a mason jar or gas can. It's wide at the top to easily capture liquid, and then it guides that liquid into a tighter space as it goes down. A "Marketing Funnel" represents the stages of your relationship with new customers. You start with advertising to a big audience at the top of the funnel. As the relationships get more serious, the size of the audience gets smaller and they move down the funnel, until they become customers.

GET A WIDER REACH

When the ad targeting and marketing funnel are both dialed in, then you can pour some gas on the fire with a bigger ad budget, getting your ads in front of more people.

Around The Campfire

THE DOORWAY TO GROWTH

Not all modern marketing campaigns involve digital ads. My favorite unconventional story from this trail is about a custom door manufacturer. As a family business, the founder passed the mantle to his children. They were ready to bring fresh energy and ideas to the business, beginning with marketing.

The business had been built entirely on lumber yard relationships for decades. They had a rudimentary catalog that was given to lumber yards to help homeowners pick doors for their new custom home. However, their old catalog was very technical and confusing. The manufacturer could literally build any door that a homeowner or designer could dream up, and the combinations were nearly infinite. It was simply overwhelming for customers to decide what to buy.

The new sibling management team knew that if the lumber yard sales representatives were taken care of, the customers would be able to make product decisions, and their business would grow. So, they hired a design agency that completely rebranded their company, keeping the same name and same products, but providing a fresh modern look that welcomed homeowners. They knew that showing off actual examples of doors rather than merely line drawings would be key to helping homeowners make decisions, so they also invested in photography.

In all, the new owners now had a fresh look with compelling photos and a brand-new catalog that was reorganized to make design decisions easy, with plenty of real-life examples of their doors. They also took the catalog online, which hadn't previously been done. The website was built in a similar fashion, with ease-of-use being the number one goal.

All of this effort resulted in an immediate 30% rise in sales that continued on. They expanded production from two shifts to three, working around the clock. It turned out that they didn't need to do any other marketing as long as the lumberyards stayed stocked with catalogs. This one-time investment paid off repeatedly and maxed out their production.

Caution Signs

If you don't have measurable goals, you are doomed to overspend. In marketing speak they're often referred to as "Key Performance Indicators" (KPI). What is the one metric that is most important to your marketing campaign, the primary yard stick to measure success by? Is it traffic to your website? Inbound phone calls? New sales of this product or that service? Overall revenue? Net profit? Make sure you know what is most important before you begin, and be certain that you can measure and report it with accuracy.

With marketing campaigns, you can overspend in a hurry. Be careful with what you spend, along with where and when you spend it. Efficiency is key, and it takes time and attention to accomplish that.

Make sure your operations can handle new sales. A successful campaign that exceeds your expectations can overburden your team on this trail, creating busy work or bloating your overhead. Make sure it's sustainably profitable new business that's coming in.

Preparation

Am I spending the right amount on advertising?

Am I you targeting too broadly or too tightly?

Have I experimented with different ad messaging?

Is the Call To Action clear and frictionless?

Can we quickly service new leads?

How much would I pay per lead? How much should I? What is the market rate?

Can I report Return On Investment (ROI) from ad spend all the way down to profit?

The Trailhead

Start by clarifying your value proposition in your advertising. Figure out what your offering really means to your audience and how it changes their life. Make sure your Call To Action is easy to understand and complete. Once you have dialed in these aspects of your campaign, double down on your advertising budget. Report the results and review to keep a close eye on your ROI.

Your Sherpa

BRANDING & MARKETING AGENCY

There are plenty of talented agencies that are friendly to small business marketing campaigns. Agencies will have experience in particular sectors, so seek out one that has worked with a business like yours already.

Trail Markers

Your marketing metrics (or KPI) will tell the story of success on this trail. Examples include traffic numbers, conversion rates, and sales totals. It's best if those metrics lead all the way to profit, and then you can just watch the bottom line on your Profit and Loss statement each month.

The Same Product
For A New Audience

LENGTH: DAY HIKE

DIFFICULTY: CLASS 1

ELEVATION GAIN: ALPINE

The Overlook

You may have another audience who would absolutely love what you have to offer, but don't know that you even exist.

This trail is about rethinking who your best audiences really are – not just who your best audience is right now.

If you are like most small businesses then you probably know your current audience well: where they live, what music they like, what transportation they prefer, how they talk, how they walk, how they vote, and maybe even how they wear their hair. But what can happen when you have your "Target Audience" archetype defined in such detail is that you forget that other people exist… other people who might love what you do.

A simple pivot to speak to a new audience can be a game changer for you. It may even be possible to offer the exact same product catalog or suite of services, with the same employees, from the same location – just to a different audience.

The Routes

TARGET A NEW DEMOGRAPHIC

"Demographic" began as an adjective but has evolved into a noun in the marketing world. Demographics might be grouped by age, gender, ethnicity, economics, or all of the above.

EXPAND YOUR GEOGRAPHY

Every successful business works well in a specific geographic area. Could you offer the same product or service to another audience outside of that geography? For example, if you are urban then you can expand into rural or suburban areas.

EXPLORE PSYCHOGRAPHICS

Psychographics are the next level of Demographics. Now you're grouping people with similar opinions, taste, attitudes, or values. Even within the same demographic and geography, you can have very different Psychographics.

Around The Campfire

THE YOUTUBE CONNECTION

Before YouTube became a household name it was a video dating site. People who were looking to get a date were able to post videos of themselves, describing who they are and what they're looking for in a mate. The only problem was… nobody used it! The novel technology allowing users to upload and publish their own videos had been built, but the brand didn't have a good audience.

The founders made the decision to scrap the dating concept and open the platform up. Anybody could now post any video for any reason and share it with the world. They expanded their demographic from single adults to the general public and sold for over a billion dollars the very next year.[16]

TREEHUGGERS, REDNECKS & THE GREAT OUTDOORS

I love camping. Waking up in the great outdoors with fresh air and songbirds, getting the fire going, cooking in the open air, and of course enjoying a mug of hot coffee while the sun rises. When you are camping, you realize that what we actually need in this life isn't very much. Some basic food, some basic shelter, clean water, someplace cool when it's hot, and someplace warm when it's cold.

You know who else loves camping? Treehuggers. Getting back to basics, staying in tune with nature, setting out with the absolute bare bone essentials, living outside, and enjoying every minute of it.

And who else besides that loves to camp? Rednecks. They love it for a lot of the same reasons, too. They like to be outdoors as often as possible and get back to their roots, to the way generations before them lived. Rednecks might be cooking sausage instead of quinoa and smell like tobacco instead of patchouli, but the heart behind the activity is pretty much the same. Trust me, I've camped with both!

If you are in the camping industry, then you have an opportunity to double your audience by speaking to both treehuggers and rednecks – but you must speak very differently to each audience in order to resonate and see results. You may even need two totally different brands (selling the same products) to accomplish that.

⚠️

Caution Signs

The warning with this method is to be careful about your brand. It can be tempting to try and become everything to everyone, but not even Walmart can do that. No single brand can serve everyone. So don't dilute your brand by going too generic on your messaging. If you sense that you are spreading too thin and losing your sense of purpose (and thus your impact), you may consider creating another brand to serve that new audience. You can even do this under the same company with the exact same product, service and team.

Preparation

Who would love my product that doesn't know I exist?

Could I appeal to an audience that is older, younger, more urban or suburban, a different gender, race, political affiliation, or location than my current audience?

For "Business To Consumer" (B2C): could I go "Business To Business" (B2B) and become a wholesaler?

For B2B: could I become B2C and sell direct to the end customer?

📍

The Trailhead

Clearly define your current audience, and brainstorm who would also use and love your current offerings.

Your Sherpa

BRANDING CONSULTANT

Hiring someone to help with your positioning and messaging can help you clarify what you're saying, and who you're saying it to.

Trail Markers

If you launch a new brand, then your trail markers should be easy to see. If you are pursuing new customers under the same brand, then your top line revenue should be going up on your Profit and Loss statement.

A Different Product
For The Same Audience

LENGTH: DAY HIKE

DIFFICULTY: CLASS 1

ELEVATION GAIN: ALPINE

The Overlook

If your audience already knows you and trusts you, chances are that you can sell them more products or services than you are now, with little friction. Think about the relationship that your brand has with its audience. They are living their life, and then they interact with your brand and then go back to living their life – what happens immediately before and after that interaction? That is going to be your best opportunity to grow with this trail.

Take for instance a car dealership: someone needs a car, they come in and buy a car, then they leave – but the relationship doesn't have to end right there (or be put on hold until they need another car). The customer will need regular maintenance and repair on that car, so dealerships "give" a service warranty as part of the sale… which is really an upsell that is baked into the cost of the sale. They continue to grow that relationship, which gives them "top of mind awareness" in the customer's mind. It also gives the dealership more opportunities to build trust in the brand through customer service, and most importantly it means that the relationship is fresh and strong when the customer is ready to buy another car.

Just about any business has the opportunity to do this. Think about what is happening in your customer's journey and how you fit in. How can you make their life easier, with less friction, while adding value around your current interaction with them? What did they do before they bought what you're currently offering? Keep in mind that this effort is only successful if you are truly adding value to their life.

The Routes

CREATE PRODUCT BUNDLES

Bundles are a fantastic way to introduce your customers to new products they didn't even know they needed. You can package related products or services into a discounted set and give it a catchy name.

FIND UPSELLS

Offer a good reason for people to upgrade. You can give a discount if they upgrade before a certain deadline, or you can offer social proof that the upgrade is worth it (such as testimonials). Whatever you do, make it as easy as possible for people to level up.

DEFINE CROSS-SELLS

Often there are related products that would be helpful for what your customers are already buying. If you offer a product, then you could create a service for that product such as cleaning, repair, or a warranty. And if you offer a service, you can offer a product that complements that service.

Around The Campfire

PRINCE OF P.R.

In the early 2000's, Prince was a household favorite despite not having published a hit album of new music in over a decade. In 2004, however, Prince released an album called *Musicology* which became his best-selling album in quite some time, with over half a million sales in the first 5 weeks. This was thanks in large part to his clever business tactic of including the sale of one album with each concert ticket, which sold out one arena after another.

He sold an estimated 158,000 copies of the album this way,[17] and I'm sure concertgoers were pleasantly surprised to receive a copy on entry. It feels like a bonus to them, it helped his published metrics and chart position, and it created some fantastic buzz in the critical first month of release. It even led to Billboard revising its policy for chart publishing.

You may not have an opportunity to make a sale to your audience that they didn't even know happened, but it is very likely that you can offer something else to your current audience that will help them and makes sense for you to offer.

DO YOU WANT FRIES WITH THAT?

That old familiar phrase is so deeply engrained in Americana that it even became the title of a country song. McDonalds has paved the way with many business innovations over the decades, but this is perhaps the most effective cross-sell in sales history. Most often the answer is "yes", and the question simply needs to be asked in order to add value to the customer and increase the sale price.

Think of a product or service that complements what is already being purchased. If you can find something that your customer already wants but just didn't know it, and you can introduce it in a friendly and frictionless manner, then you have a winner.

⚠️

Caution Signs

You can muddy your message with too many products if you're not careful. If your business has a bread-and-butter product that everybody knows you for, then tread lightly when offering new products. Make sure that it makes real sense for your current audience to buy your new product as well.

Preparation

What pains, needs or desires do my current customers have before and after they buy my products or services?

How can I make my current customers' lives easier and better before or after a current sale?

What products or services make sense to bundle together for customers?

The Trailhead

Clearly define your current audience. Then map out their journey, and how you fit into it now. Now dream up how you can be a closer part of their journey.

Don't just define a classic "customer journey" with you at the center, but rather define their personal journey, and what small part you currently play. Then you can see a picture for what other opportunities there are for you in that journey.

Your Sherpas

BUSINESS CONSULTANT

Fresh eyes from outside of your organization can often see opportunities that you might be overlooking.

YOUR CUSTOMERS

Getting honest and helpful insight from your best and most trusted customers can change the way you look at your business.

➡

Trail Markers

Track sales of your new product. Being able to report sales by product or category is helpful, especially on your Profit and Loss statement where you can see the entire financial picture of your business in one view, organized by month or year.

A Different Product For A New Audience

LENGTH: BACKPACKING TRIP

DIFFICULTY: CLASS 3

ELEVATION GAIN: ALPINE

The Overlook

This concept is all about reimagining the future of your business. You can stay in the same niche and leverage your expertise. Reinvent the way your business operates and increase the value it's adding to the world.

This is the "Picks and Axes" approach to your industry. During the California Gold Rush, thousands upon thousands of prospectors traveled west with every last dime they had, geared up and headed for the hills to strike it rich. Most failed, and ended up broke and tired after years of work. A few did strike gold, and even out of that bunch very few actually set up successful mining companies that flourished in the following decades. The real winners were the companies that supplied the prospectors who needed to buy picks and axes, shovels, mules, lumber, hardware, clothing, food, tents, and so on. Levi Strauss & Company was one of the winners of this era, supplying quality workwear to the folks flooding into Northern California who spent all of their money on a hope and a dream.

There are "Picks and Axes" opportunities in every industry.

The Routes

CREATE AN INFO PRODUCT

You have information that other people want. When you find yourself thinking "If I only knew that before I started this business" then you have an Info Product concept already defined. An Info Product could be as simple as a text document with industry secrets, or it can be a book, a series of emails, or a full-blown video course.

SHARE AN INDUSTRY TOOL

If you have a tool or a system that you have created to help your business succeed, then you can sell that to other businesses. It is likely that every single business like yours is facing the same challenges that you have already solved.

BUSINESS-IN-A-BOX

Most small businesses that are started won't have a 5 year anniversary. Some founders would love to buy a shortcut past all of the pitfalls you have faced in your business. Wouldn't you? You can sell your entire business methods, systems, preferred equipment, hiring practices, and more–all in one huge bundle.

SELL YOUR LEADS

Sales prospects, or "leads", are a commodity item. If you are turning away business, those contacts have value to other people who do what you do. You can negotiate a price per lead, send the leads to them as they come in to you, and then invoice them at the end of the month.

Around The Campfire

SHEDDING OVERHEAD

My favorite example of rethinking your entire business is a shed business that I learned about. The owner of the business had been building sheds for years and decided to get out of the day-to-day of construction life. I wouldn't be surprised if age, wear and tear or burnout led to this move (or all of the above!). The shed builder had years of knowledge, experience, and business tools that he decided to share with others.

So he created a "business in a box" concept, where any handyman can buy into his program and become a shed builder in their own town. They get access to all of his detailed building plans, with CAD drawings, cut sheets and assembly instructions. They also get helpful tools like spreadsheets that help you estimate your costs and price a building based on today's material costs. On top of this, he created a training video series that walks the viewer through every aspect of owning and running a successful shed building business.

He's still in the shed business, but now instead of building sheds for homeowners, he is selling information to other shed builders. He leveraged his years of sweat and toil into a beautiful info product that he created one time and can sell infinitely. This is a fantastic "Picks and Axes" business.

FROM GYM TO LAUNCHED

Alex Hormozi has built quite a name for himself as an investor and business thought leader, but it hasn't always been that way. He started his career as an entrepreneur with workout gyms. Alex was good at the gym business, but it's a grind. This became even more so when he expanded to 5 locations. He started Gym Launch as a way to help other gym owners grow their own business and was finding that he was good at it. Eventually he sold his gyms and focused on Gym Launch.

The consulting business eventually birthed a playbook, which then became a program that gym owners could follow to find success. After growing to thousands of program members nationwide, Alex sold his company for tens of millions of dollars. He pivoted from being a gym owner to being an advocate for all gym owners, and experienced a radical change in profitability.

PICKING UP THE SLACK

The Slack app has millions of business customers and has become the single leader in asynchronous business communication. But that's not how the product was designed – in fact, Slack was one of the most beautiful pivots in modern business history.

What is now the core product of Slack was merely a chat feature of a failed interactive video game. The game was a venture that the founders had raised money for and had some users. It didn't take off nearly as expected, and the company's financial runway was shrinking every day. However, the leadership team realized that people were using the game even though they weren't very excited about the playability. They started asking questions and got feedback that some users were actually only using the game to chat with their friends. As a last-ditch effort before pulling up stakes on the entire venture, they decided to repackage that part of their software as a small business product to replace Skype, ICQ and other legacy chat products that just didn't measure up. Today one of their ad slogans is "more gets done with Slack", and as a user for nearly a decade, I wholeheartedly agree.

Caution Signs

While you're building something new, you may be able to fund it with your current revenue. If that's the case, then do not ignore your main business. Keep it going strong so that your new venture has a chance to be successful.

Preparation

What information do I personally have that other people might want? How could I become their teacher or mentor?

What new products or services are my team capable of producing? (Make a list.)

How can I leverage my expertise to help others? If I knew what I know now when I first started in the business, how would that have changed my journey?

Do I have systems or processes that are
better than others in the industry?

The Trailhead

Start with yourself. Define your assets and expertise.

Your Sherpas

BUSINESS CONSULTANT

An outsider without blinders on can help you identify unique assets that you might be taking for granted. This person can have experience in your industry or not. It can help to have fresh eyes.

PEERS

It can also help to get a fresh perspective from a fellow business owner, even if they're not in the same space as you. Having a business peer group can cover your blind spots.

Trail Markers

Taking this trail could mean a big pivot, which may even need to be a different brand or a new company. Whichever way you go, make sure you can track your sales.

Vertical Integration

LENGTH: BACKPACKING TRIP

DIFFICULTY: CLASS 3

ELEVATION GAIN: SUMMIT

The Overlook

Growth by acquiring or forming other companies can be a great way to see immediate growth, if it's planned and executed well. This is "big risk, big reward" territory. In terms of trails, it's the skinny little goat trail with a thousand-foot drop and loose rocks, but at the end is the most spectacular summit you could ever imagine.

Vertical Integration is when you acquire (or become) a supplier or customer of your current business. It is growth via supply chain. The most common way that a small business Vertically Integrates is by buying a building rather than leasing space, but there are likely many other creative ways to also take this trail for your business.

You have the opportunity for both businesses to benefit right away when you're Vertically Integrating. Typically the downstream business (the one closer to the end customer), will get better products, terms or service. Meanwhile the upstream business will get a reliable customer relationship. When you bolt together two businesses like this, it opens up a lot of options for growth on both ends.

The Routes

BECOME YOUR OWN SUPPLIER

You can start a new business that becomes a supplier of your current business. You can also look for a business to buy.

BECOME YOUR OWN CUSTOMER

You can start or buy a business that becomes a customer of your current business for an immediate boost in revenue.

BECOME YOUR OWN LANDLORD

It's very common for long-time business tenants to buy the building they lease. Owners who do this will often keep the building when they sell their business, having a stable tenant already in place.

Around The Campfire

INTEGRATION ROCKS

One of my favorite examples of vertical integration in a small business is about a hardscape installation company in Texas. They built patios, walkways, planters and so on out of stone and brick, mostly serving suburban homes. It started out as a side hustle for the owner, who was managing jobs and crews when he was in town from his full-time traveling job.

It grew to the point where he could work on the hardscape business full time, and he really put the pedal to the metal. The business grew to a point where he was limited by his suppliers. Frustrated with endless promises and lackluster delivery, he was determined to do it better – so he opened his own stone supply company. This was no small task, but to him it would be worth the effort, because he would be able to serve his installation business well, and also serve the rest of the market (in other words, his competition), because his current suppliers would be so easy to beat if someone just outworked them.

Before long, he found out where the real source of the industry's pains came from: the stone quarries. It turned out that the quarries that supply all of the stone products to the entire region had a long history of overpromising, and then delivering late or messing up orders. On a quest to redeem the supply chain, he began looking into quarries, and eventually bought one that produced the most common type of stone he used in projects. Now his yard store gets the first and best pick of the product, and his installation company gets the first and best from the store – and he can control all of the turnaround times.

What I love about that story is that the end customer, the homeowner, is the heart of the entire effort. Now this owner's chain of businesses are running on all cylinders and dominating his market – but it was quite a toil to get it there. Everything he did was so that his homeowner customers would get stone projects done on time and on budget.

FROM SEED TO SHADE

Another great example of vertical integration in small business is a story about a tree farm that I had the pleasure to work with. Their story mirrors the hardscape company, and they both grew around the same time, in the same area. Once upon a time a man had a landscaping company. He started by mowing yards by himself, which grew to several crews, which then grew to landscape maintenance. As he and his team did good work and earned the trust of his customers, he started getting requests to do bigger and bigger landscape projects, eventually getting into tree planting as well.

It turns out that trees are a whole different ballgame, but he was up for the challenge. As he kept saying "yes" to more tree jobs, he grew frustrated with the lack of quality and service in the tree industry. As he looked into it, he realized that his "tree farms" were really retail lots that were buying trees from actual farms that were growing them.

So what did he do? He started a tree retail company, naturally! He saw an opportunity to shine in an industry where poor service was commonplace. And it worked. At a certain point he found a similar issue to the hardscape company though, where his tree farm suppliers were overpromising and under-delivering to the retail lots, which trickled down throughout the entire ecosystem all the way to the homeowner's experience. He knew that building a farm was his destiny.

After finding the right land, he began planting trees for the future. That's when he found another broken piece to the system, which was the seed market. The biggest retailers get first choice to the seeds, leaving little guys like him to sort through the leftovers. Trees are a slow game, but over the decades he built the entire supply chain and now offers the highest quality seeds and the best trees.

FOOTBALL FOODIES

Jerry Jones, the owner of the Dallas Cowboys football club, has grown his empire even bigger by creating a food service company called Legends Hospitality. It services all food concessions at every new NFL stadium that has been built since 2009. That company is now worth over a billion dollars,[18] and has been quietly growing in the shadow of the football franchise.

BANKING ON BOXING

Big-time boxing matches are typically put together by a promoter, who acts as the bank and the marketing outfit – much like how a record label is to a musician. However, they tend to take a huge cut of the fight. Often the boxers do pretty well themselves just on the prize money, but that's a small piece of a huge pie. Champion boxer Floyd Mayweather vertically integrated by creating a promotion company. Now, in addition to the boxing prize money, Floyd "Money" Mayweather also wins from the ticket sales and pay-per-view rights to all of his fights.

ACES TO AGENCY

Roger Federer is perhaps the most decorated tennis player to play the game. He won 103 singles tournaments in his career, including 20 majors. In 2017 he created a representation company with his agent to change the way that athletes are advocated for in brand partnership deals.[19]

Sports agents negotiate contracts both on and off the court, and typically keep 10% of the athlete's contract earnings. That is often worth millions of dollars per client. As a top-tier athlete, he could design the type of agent relationship that he wanted to have, and also take part in that huge commission. He could also leverage his professional relationships to recruit athletes into his agency, which now represents not just tennis players but athletes from other sports as well.

Caution Signs

This is not an easy trail. A bad deal can handcuff both businesses if you're not careful. You need to make sure that you are not overpaying for a business, and that your financing terms are friendly to your current cashflow.

In my experience, when a new owner takes over a business the sales tend to drop right away. Then it's up to their smarts, ambition, effort, and intuition to get customers to buy into the new ownership. When forecasting the finances of your deal, expect sales to drop shortly after acquisition.

◫

Preparation

What suppliers do I pay the most money to?

Which suppliers would be the easiest to own and operate?

Are there any customers that are facing big life changes?

Are there any customers whose business could grow with a few simple changes?

◉

The Trailhead

Begin by making a list of all of your biggest suppliers (including your landlord). Then make a list of all of your best customers. Identify the businesses on each list that are most realistic to buy, or start a competing business.

You can do an online search for businesses for sale as well. People buy and sell businesses every day. Then it can become a new suppliers or customer for the business that you have now.

Your Sherpas

BUSINESS BROKER

You will want to go with a broker who is experienced in the size of deal that you're doing.

ACCOUNTANT

A good accountant who is versed in business transactions can help you identify the health of a prospective business you're taking a serious look at.

Trail Markers

The Trail Markers should be easy to spot on this trail. The new business(es) you acquire should have separate books, so you can review the Profit and Loss statements from before and after the acquisition to gauge success.

Horizontal Integration

LENGTH: BACKPACKING TRIP

DIFFICULTY: CLASS 3

ELEVATION GAIN: SUMMIT

The Overlook

Simply put, Horizontal Integration is growth by acquiring competitors. It can be more nuanced than that, but in most cases it would mean simply buying a competitor and merging the businesses together.

Horizontal Integration is a long game with a long-range return on investment, but it can be a fantastic way to grow your business – especially if you've really "figured it out". If you have a competitive advantage, if you have better marketing, sales or operations, if you have a more notable or trustworthy brand than your competition, then this trail will be a great way to add value to an acquisition right away. You get their book of business, their supplier relationships, existing customers and their team, and you can apply the strengths of your business to all of that to make both of them better.

Now the idea is nice, but the execution of this trail can be tricky. First off, if you have a contentious relationship with your competitors then that creates a major hurdle right away. You may need to look outside of your region for a good business to buy. Even then, it's a tricky conversation to start. In the business broker world, they say that people aren't ready to sell their business until they encounter one of the "Three D's": Death, Disease, or Divorce. I have also heard of Disenchantment, Dullness, Distress, Departure, and Disagreement being added to that list.

Even if you find a business that's ready to sell and you close the deal, you need to tread lightly and be very smart about how you merge them together. It's often the case that you will have to let some employees go from either side, and you want to be careful about switching brands on the new business' customer base. They will already have questions of trust with the ownership changing hands, and you can really rock the boat by making too many changes too quickly. Treat those customers as a flight risk until you have proven to them that you can add value and make their lives better.

A "Roll Up" strategy is a common way to grow your business by way of this trail. If you have a strong brand and solid operations, then you can seek out similar businesses that are weak where you're strong and roll them up into your business. This typically involves rebranding the new company as your brand and implementing your Standard Operating Procedures into their crew.

If you have successfully taken this trail all the way to the summit, what you will see in the long run is a single business that has grown faster than you ever could by simply increasing your marketing spend. You may have even learned a few tricks along the way that you would not have otherwise discovered: new methods, processes, philosophies, perspectives or even found new suppliers to work with.

The Routes

BUY A COMPETITOR

This is the trickiest route on the trail, but if it is navigated well you could dominate your local market in one stroke of the pen.

BUY A SIMILAR BUSINESS IN A NEW AREA

This move is a shortcut to Trail #7 (More Of The Same Product To A Different Audience), you just have to pay admission instead of going out on your own. Expanding your geographic footprint by acquiring a business in a new area is a fantastic growth strategy, and both businesses typically benefit. You will immediately have double the intel, supplier relationships, negotiation leverage, systems and processes, and customer base.

BUY A BIGGER OR SMALLER BUSINESS

You can immediately level-up your business or the business you are buying if you buy right. Identify areas that you are strong and weak in and look for businesses to buy that are the opposite: strong where you are weak, and weak where you are strong.

Around The Campfire

VIDEO GAMING

Blockbuster Video was deeply a part of American culture in the 1980's and 90's. The latest movies lined the walls, along with your favorite classics, video games, even popcorn and candy were all handy for some Friday night fun. Blockbuster had over 9,000 locations in its day, and it accomplished that by "Rolling Up" mom-and-pop video stores into the Blockbuster brand. They took this trail into the stratosphere before they were left behind by the digital age.

GRASS AND GROWTH

I helped a fantastic lawn care company grow their brand and their business through Horizontal Integration. Lawn care tends to attract single owner/operators, who work really hard to grow their business. They are "Head Chef and Chief Bottle Washer", as the saying goes. While they might be good at the craft of lawn care, they're often weak in marketing, accounting, and organization.

This Roll-Up company makes owner/operators an offer that they can't refuse to buy their business and bring it under one brand. The seller becomes a manager, gets paid fairly well and doesn't have to do all of the business admin tasks that they weren't any good at anyway. The seller's customers keep the relationship with the seller, but get to experience a new brand. The seller/manager gets to leverage the company's enterprise-quality tools and operate within the new Standard Operating Procedures, which have been shaped and perfected over time.

It's a win-win-win for all parties involved (including the customers) and helps the lawn care brand grow by leaps and bounds with each acquisition.

⚠

Caution Signs

Buying a business means that you and the seller both need to get really cozy with each other. This can be uncomfortable, to say the least. You will both be making yourselves vulnerable by sharing your finances, and the seller might have to take a big risk in letting a competitor behind the curtain of the business during the due diligence process. Be cautious and empathetic as you take this trail.

Like Vertical Integration, you will face challenges when mashing your businesses together, except with Horizontal Integration there might be some more dynamics to navigate. If you buy a direct competitor, many times the employees already dislike each other because they have a tribal mentality. This may even be from your own doing. If you're not careful about the integration, it might feel to your employees as though you have invited the enemy to move into camp. Culture can be difficult to manage and is an art form in itself.

Preparation

Is one of my competitors going through a major life-changing event?

Have I had an eye on another business in the area?

Am I ready to buy another business like mine?

The Trailhead

Begin down this trail by studying your competitors. A helpful strategy is to look just outside of your service area for opportunities, which allows you to not only bring the strengths of your business together with the new one, but also expands your geographic footprint as well.

You can also do an online search for businesses for sale, which will pull up several popular listing websites that business brokers use to get the word out.

Your Sherpa

BUSINESS BROKER

Even if you already have a target business in mind, you can hire a broker to help guide you through each step of the merger, including the valuation and securing the financing.

➡

Trail Markers

With a Roll Up, your business will be buying the assets of another business. The "assets" could include branding, marketing, customer lists, employees, equipment, or operations and procedures. Regardless of how the deal is technically structured, you will want to set up clear reporting in your books. Sales and profit should be easy to track in the new business.

PROFIT HIKER

Booking Your Trip

If you've made it this far, then you've almost certainly decided to take one of these 11 trails. When should you do it, and how long should it take?

That answer depends entirely on your specific situation. Now you have the trail map and know where the trailhead is, it's up to you to take the journey. The hike, the trail and the hiker will always be different, but the hiking process is always the same. Here are the steps a hiker needs to take in order to embark on a new journey:

1. Study the trails
2. Pick a trail
3. Prepare for the hike
4. Find the trailhead
5. Start hiking

You might have some ideas cooking already about a trail, inspired by the journeys that other businesses have taken. If so, that's fantastic – don't lose this mental momentum. Pick that trail and start planning.

A quick win can put wind in your sails. There is a human response called "Completion Bias", where we gain mental momentum by completing tasks.[20] When you have a big project at hand, you might tackle a small task right off the bat just to feel the sensation of accomplishment before starting on the larger, longer, or more complicated tasks. Dave Ramsey agrees with this approach in his "Debt Snowball" strategy for paying off small debts before tackling large debts, even though it might make more sense financially to do the opposite.[21] Sam Parr, the founder of The Hustle and Hampton, also agrees. Sam says that achievable goals are more inspiring than big, lofty goals because achievement creates momentum.[22] Don't fight Completion Bias, rather use it to your advantage.

One of these trails is sure to stick out above the rest of them, so start there, and commit to hiking it. By the time you're done with that hike, you'll be more prepared to approach the next one.

Even if you already have a particular trail in mind, you should take time to consider each and every one of these trails for your business. Trust the process. If one of the trails sounds ridiculous or unattainable at first, give it time and attention to study the trail and think about what that hike looks like for you. You might be surprised what ideas you uncover.

Here is a look at all of the trails with their respective Trail Ratings…

Trail Rating Chart

NAME	LENGTH	DIFFICULTY	ELEVATION
Trail #1: Raise Prices	Scenic Loop	Class 1	Alpine
Trail #2: Reduce Costs	Scenic Loop	Class 2	Foothill
Trail #3: Turn Overhead Into A Profit Center	Backpacking Trip	Class 3	Alpine
Trail #4: Optimize	Day Hike	Class 2	Alpine
Trail #5: Automate	Day Hike	Class 2	Alpine
Trail #6: The Same Product For More Of The Same Audience	Scenic Loop	Class 1	Foothill
Trail #7: The Same Product For A New Audience	Day Hike	Class 1	Alpine
Trail #8: A Different Product For The Same Audience	Day Hike	Class 1	Alpine
Trail #9: A Different Product For A New Audience	Backpacking Trip	Class 3	Alpine
Trail #10: Vertical Integration	Backpacking Trip	Class 3	Summit
Trail #11: Horizontal Integration	Backpacking Trip	Class 3	Summit

Don't get hung up on how long you're spending on any of these trails – to quote some classic advice from a really obscure movie titled *Escanaba In Da Moonlight*: "If a job's worth doing, it's worth doing right". Spend the right amount of time on it, not more or less. Only you can know how much that should be.

Once you have a trail identified, take the time to lay out a plan of action. Don't oversimplify or overcomplicate it. Break it down into a few milestones that you can measure up to. Then create the tasks that you will need to accomplish those. Use your existing frameworks to help you accomplish it – if you're a Post-It Note user, then use them. If you set alarms or use notes on your phone, do that. If you use a project management system to tackle your day, put your tasks into the system. However you tend to get things done now, leverage that same method to help you hike your trail.

Then it's time to find the trailhead–the starting point–and get hiking. At this point, your hike takes whatever it takes. Be diligent and stay the course. Remain committed to action more than accomplishment. When you are hiking, you just need to keep placing one foot in front of the other, even when you don't want to. This matters more than anything else on a hike. It's what gets you there, and what gets you home. If you do this, then accomplishment will take care of itself!

Making Room For Your Journey

The first step of your journey is to study. There are 11 trails, so here is what I recommend for you. Give each trail one full hour a day, for the next 2 weeks. Commit to 11 full hours of trail studying to change the future of your business forever. Treat each trail like it might be the one to unlock greatness. Create space to explore each idea to its fullest. Get creative.

As a creative professional, I have come to believe that everybody is made in the image of their Creator. Even if you don't see yourself as creative, you are. People who have told me they are not creative are also coming up with new recipes for amazing dinners, crafting weekly class content for their students to learn in new and engaging ways, or reorganizing the way that hospitals work. We all have creativity built in us, and you can use that skill to reimagine your business. You are creative! If you are not familiar with how to tap into that force of your nature, then try what I call "Active Creative Meditation".

What I have learned is that if you establish a playground for your creativity, then your brain is free to connect dots that you may not have even known were there. So what you need to do is quiet yourself on a regular basis and then give your creativity permission to go wild. This is a simple yet powerful tool for your business, and as a small business owner it's your responsibility to make space in your life for creativity and the reimagining of your future.

Active Creative Meditation

Traditional meditation can be a great way to quiet your mind and focus on the challenge ahead. It is a fantastic tool for well being, and a great thing to weave into everyday life – but that doesn't personally work for my own creativity. What does work for me is a repetitive physical task like jogging, cycling, fishing, or swimming. Each of these have a "best" version for this creative exercise.

For example…

Fly fishing a river is one of the most meditative physical activities I have ever done. Fly fishing gives my mind the space to be creative (now that I have the basics down!). Compare that to fishing on a deep-sea tuna boat, which is an exciting and highly engaged activity, requiring all of your mental energy and attention. They're both fishing, but only one is helpful for this process. Slow, repetitious fishing is fertile ground for Active Creative Meditation.

Cycling on a stationary bike in a gym is a fantastic environment for Active Creative Meditation. The repetition of the activity combined with an elevated heart rate can push creative thinking into overdrive. Compare that to bombing down a steep mountain bike trail, navigating ruts, rocks, and trees while adrenaline is coursing through every vein. It's exciting, mind-bending, and borderline addictive–but it's not even close to being a fertile environment for creative thinking.

The same goes for jogging or swimming. Jogging in a busy city with taxis, busses and pedestrians swirling all around you requires intense focus on your environment. Jogging on a quiet trail takes that burden from your mind and can transition your mental capacity over to your creative mind. Swimming in an ocean can also be exciting, with wind, waves and tide requiring mental focus. Compare that to swimming laps in a pool–my favorite activity for Active Creative Meditation–which gives you a simple tile stripe to follow, even freeing your mind from what you can look at.

Road trips can be a great environment for reimagining your life. There is something about breaking your daily routine, exploring new places and the endless open highway that creates an incubator for fresh ideas. In fact, the idea to write this book arrived on a road trip!

While I like to use physical redundancy to activate my creative mind, others may prefer a little more chaos. You might like to have the TV on in the background to focus or prefer to be surrounded by lots of activity such as a coffee shop. Conversely, a day at the spa might be the ticket for you to get in the right mind space. Or you might try a mobile app for mental focus that emits particular noise patterns to promote deep thinking.

Where and *how* you decide to start your journey should matter to you personally. You know yourself best, so make note of your strengths and then leverage those natural tendencies for creativity. Create a place that you can study these trails intently, with a clear head and open mind.

Group Hikes

Hiking is better together! Connecting with other business owners and hiking a trail together has so many benefits. More hikers make trailside navigation easier. You can point out pitfalls to one other as you come across them. Groups can also help an injured hiker get back to safety when they would have been completely stuck on their own.

There is also the benefit of accountability which can be a huge advantage to a small business owner. It's a positive version of peer pressure that keeps everybody on track because we don't want to let down our fellow hikers. Hiking together can lead you to accomplish more together than you would have done on your own. Surrounding yourself with a solid group of peers tends to bring out your full potential.

I have been a part of several small entrepreneur or business owner meetups throughout the years and it can be tremendously helpful to lean on others who are traveling the same journey. Assemble a small group of like-minded Profit Hikers to meet regularly and help each other out.

Don't overlook the perk of companionship in a group hike. Loneliness is an epidemic, and the antidote is community among your peers. A study performed by BYU professor of psychology and neuroscience Julianne Holt-Lunstad, PhD found "loneliness and social isolation are twice as harmful to physical and mental health as obesity".[23] According to Forbes nearly 30% of business owners and the self-employed regard loneliness as a notable problem in their life.[24] If you are in that camp then it's up to you to do something about it. Start with a group hike.

Your Feet And The Peak

When you are hiking a trail there are times that you need to watch your step. Rocks, ruts, roots, and ridges can turn a leisurely hike into a medical emergency. But if you spend the entire hike staring at your feet you will miss the things that matter. Scenic views and memorable moments with fellow hikers are what it's all about.

The same is true in your Profit Hiker journey. There are times when you need to watch your steps and be focused on tactical micro-movements to avoid a catastrophic injury. But don't forget to gaze at the peak. That is your destination. Any time the trail allows for it, take your eyes off your feet and look around. A successful hike requires both micro and macro perspectives, and also has a regular cadence of switching between the two.

Check Your Backtrail

If a hiking trail is not well marked, it is wise for hikers to check their backtrail periodically. This is because the trail looks very different walking the opposite direction. If you lose the trail, you will ideally have some mental photos (or actual photos) to reference so that you can identify landmarks and find the trail again.

As a Profit Hiker, you should also check your backtrail so that you don't lose your way. Remind yourself of where you've been and what you've accomplished.

Hikers often create "cairns" which are small rock piles to reassure other hikers that they are on the right path. These cairns also serve as a monument to prior success. Build some cairns along your trail to mark your accomplishments. Celebrate all your wins, even the small ones. When you go to check your backtrail, you will see the cairns along the trailside that prove that what you're doing is worth the effort and encourage you to keep going.

What Are You Waiting For?

You have your trail maps, you have studied the trails, you have prepared for the journey, and you know where the trailhead is. It's time to start hiking.

You are a Profit Hiker – so what is the next mountain you will climb?

Sources

1. Air Traffic By The Numbers. Federal Aviation Administration. [Online] April 10, 2023. [Cited: November 9, 2023.] https://www.faa.gov/air_traffic/by_the_numbers.

2. Bieber, Christy. Revealing Divorce Statistics In 2023. Forbes Advisor. [Online] August 8, 2023. [Cited: November 9, 2023.] https://www.forbes.com/advisor/legal/divorce/divorce-statistics/.

3. State of the Global Workplace: 2023 Report. Gallup. [Online] [Cited: November 9, 2023.] https://www.gallup.com/workplace/349484/state-of-the-global-workplace.aspx.

4. Statistics on U.S. Generosity. Philanthropy Roundtable. [Online] [Cited: November 1, 2022.] https://www.philanthropyroundtable.org/resource/statistics-on-u-s-generosity.

5. Workplace gift inspires and uplifts employee. YouTube. [Online] May 19, 2019. [Cited: November 9, 2023.] https://www.youtube.com/watch?v=Zv97n5a-6qI&t=4s.

6. Acuff, Jon. LinkedIn. [Online] [Cited: November 9, 2023.] https://www.linkedin.com/posts/jonacuff_a-few-weeks-ago-i-took-my-oldest-daughter-activity-6974040758265806848-kzEW/.

7. Chronic stress puts your health at risk. Mayo Clinic. [Online] [Cited: November 9, 2023.] https://www.mayoclinic.org/healthy-lifestyle/stress-management/in-depth/stress/art-20046037.

8. What is Stress? American Institute of Stress. [Online] [Cited: November 9, 2023.] https://www.stress.org/daily-life.

9. O'Connell, Brian. 8 Best Warren Buffett Quotes of All Time. U.S. News & World Report. [Online] November 14, 2023. [Cited: November 17, 2023.] https://money.usnews.com/investing/articles/best-warren-buffett-quotes-of-all-time.

10. Meyersohn, Nathaniel. Surprise: Dollar Tree's $1.25 price strategy is actually working. CNN. [Online] November 23, 2022. [Cited: November 9, 2023.] https://www.cnn.com/2022/11/23/business/dollar-tree-prices/index.html.

11. Martin, Hugo. United Airlines saves 170,000 gallons of fuel by using lighter paper on inflight magazine. Los Angeles Times. [Online] January 20, 2018. [Cited: November 9, 2023.] https://www.latimes.com/business/la-fi-travel-briefcase-united-inflight-magazine-20180120-story.html.

12. Global Study Confirms Influential Theory Behind Loss Aversion. Columbia University Mailman School of Public Health. [Online] May 18, 2020. [Cited: November 9, 2023.] https://www.publichealth.columbia.edu/news/global-study-confirms-influential-theory-behind-loss-aversion.

13. Ford Charcoal Briquets. The Henry Ford. [Online] [Cited: November 9, 2023.] https://www.thehenryford.org/collections-and-research/digital-collections/expert-sets/101417.

14. How to Escape the Hourly Rate Trap as a Coach. Business Made Simple with Donald Miller.

15. Keehler, John. Marketing Frameworks To Help You Get More Patients. Forbes. [Online] July 6, 2021. [Cited: November 9, 2023.] https://www.forbes.com/sites/forbesagencycouncil/2021/07/06/marketing-frameworks-to-help-you-get-more-patients/.

16. Dredge, Stuart. YouTube was meant to be a video-dating website. The Guardian. [Online] March 16, 2016. [Cited: November 9, 2023.] https://www.theguardian.com/technology/2016/mar/16/youtube-past-video-dating-website.

17. Billboard' Sours On Prince's Musicology Sales Experiment. MTV. [Online] May 28, 2004. [Cited: November 9, 2023.] https://www.mtv.com/news/lf7vdg/billboard-sours-on-princes-musicology-sales-experiment.

18. DiFurio, Dom. Deal to sell majority stake in Legends Hospitality hangs a $1.3 billion value on the Cowboys-backed venture. The Dallas Morning News. [Online] 1 12, 2021. [Cited: 11 9, 2023.] https://www.dallasnews.com/business/local-

companies/2021/01/12/deal-to-sell-majority-stake-in-legends-hospitality-hangs-a-13-billion-value-on-the-cowboys-backed-venture/.

19. Chai, Sanibel. Roger Federer Launches Management Firm with His Agent . Bleacher Report. [Online] December 12, 2013. [Cited: November 9, 2023.] https://bleacherreport.com/articles/1887134-federer-launches-management-firm-with-his-agent.

20. Gino, Francesca and Staats, Bradley. Your Desire to Get Things Done Can Undermine Your Effectiveness. Harvard Business Review. [Online] March 22, 2016. [Cited: November 9, 2023.] https://hbr.org/2016/03/your-desire-to-get-things-done-can-undermine-your-effectiveness.

21. How the Debt Snowball Method Works. Ramsey Solutions. [Online] October 20, 2023. [Cited: November 9, 2023.] https://www.ramseysolutions.com/debt/how-the-debt-snowball-method-works.

22. CEO Lessons: Bulls**t Mission Statements, Firing People & Saying 'NO' . My First Million.

23. Novotney, Amy. The risks of social isolation. American Psychological Association. [Online] May 2019. [Cited: November 9, 2023.] https://www.apa.org/monitor/2019/05/ce-corner-isolation.

24. Agarwal, Pragya. It Is Time We Acknowledged Loneliness In Entrepreneurs And Did Something About It. Forbes. [Online] July 12, 2018. [Cited: November 9, 2023.] https://www.forbes.com/sites/pragyaagarwaleurope/2018/07/12/loneliness-as-an-entrepreneur-heres-something-we-can-do-about-it/.

About The Author

Simon Trask's personal motto is "Creativity Meets Commerce." A graphic designer by trade, he has learned business ownership and leadership through experience.

Simon Trask is a small business owner, advisor, and advocate. His passion is to see small businesses grow notably and sustainably, because they are the heart and soul of every community.

For Simon, small businesses keep small towns full of life and character. They are also the first to step up when funds need to be raised for a local cause. "Main Street" empowers individuals to unplug from the Wall Street corporate machine.

Simon is married to Cindy, and they are raising their three children in Texas.